SELLING
FOR PEOPLE WHO
HATE TO SELL

SELLING
FOR PEOPLE WHO
HATE TO SELL

Everyday Selling Skills
for the Rest of Us

Brigid McGrath Massie

with John K. Waters

PRIMA PUBLISHING

PRIMA PUBLISHING and colophon are registered trademarks of Prima Communications, Inc.

Library of Congress Cataloging-in-Publication Data

Massie, Brigid McGrath, 1950–
    Selling for people who hate to sell: everyday selling skills for the rest of us/ Brigid McGrath Massie.
        p.cm.
    Includes index.
    ISBN 1-7615-0665-9
    1. Selling   I. Title
HF5438.25.M3739 1996
658.85-dc20   96-17507
                                                            CIP

96 97 98 99 AA 10 9 8 7 6 5 4 3 2
Printed in the United States of America

HOW TO ORDER

Single copies may be ordered from Prima Publishing, P.O. Box 1260BK, Rocklin, CA 95677; telephone (916) 632-4400. Quantity discounts are also available. On your letterhead, include information concerning the intended use of the books and the number of books you wish to purchase.

Visit us online at http://www.primapublishing.com

*To Dan, Andrea Michelle, and
Kevin Daniel,
my constant sources of joy
and inspiration.*

CONTENTS

INTRODUCTION

As I walked up to the main reception desk at the company's corporate office complex, I was greeted by a smartly dressed young man who welcomed me with a warm smile and escorted me to the elevators. I was there to speak to 200 employees and give a one-day seminar called "Personal Selling Skills for Today's Challenging Business Climate." We arrived at the fifth-floor conference rooms set aside for the seminar, and the young man turned to go.

"Won't you be attending the seminar today?" I asked him.

"Oh, no," he replied with barely hidden contempt, "I'm not in *sales*."

I was cool. "I see. Well, what do you do?"

"I'm in customer service," he said proudly. He beamed his warm smile at me again, then headed back down the hall toward the elevators.

"It's a dirty job, junior," I muttered to his smartly dressed back, "but somebody's got to do it."

I suppose I should be a little more thick skinned after nearly two decades of helping people develop the skills to do something as vile and depraved as *selling*. (How *do* I live with myself!) Still, attitudes like that young man's never fail to get to me. Though his unspoken opinion is all too common, I'm always a little shocked and more than a little saddened when I'm reminded that the threadbare stereotypes of the larcenous used car dealer and the pushy insurance man have rooted themselves so deeply into our collective psyche.

The truth is, we're *all* in sales. The problem is, many of us don't realize what that means.

The results of effective selling are clearly quantitative— more money, promotions, success—but they're also *qualitative*. When you know what you're doing and you do it well, your job is more enjoyable, easier, and more meaningful. And as you begin to think of yourself as a success, greater success just naturally follows.

This book is about the success that comes with effective, purposeful selling in everyday situations. But it's not full of the same old tricks and tactics you've seen in countless other books: no smile training, no slogans. It's not that I'm particularly squeamish about the nuts and bolts of selling. On a certain level, a sale is a sale. But manipulation never has been what selling is about for me. And besides, I didn't write this book to perpetuate stereotypes or to teach people how to steal with a clean conscience. What I've tried to do is fill these pages with sound, commonsense advice and real-world examples from my years as a professional salesperson, sales trainer, and speaker. And I've tried to do it with integrity and a genuine concern for the guy on the business end of your sales pitch.

Unlike most other publications on this subject, this book was written specifically with the nonsalesperson in mind—that is, all those folks out there, like the young man mentioned earlier, who *believe* they're not in sales.

This book is also about developing a highly valuable and transferable set of skills. In the past two decades, the American workplace has evolved into a singularly uncertain place. Changing technologies and shifting markets make it tough to find solid footing. Studies show that the average American negotiating this rough terrain will have about seven careers in his or her lifetime. The single constant in that mercurial mass is *sales*. As I see it, the ability to sell is truly a modern *survival* skill, second only, in my opinion, to the ability to learn.

The ideas put forth in these pages require clear, deliberate thinking. Therefore, this book is also about having a purpose, getting out of your own way, and getting the most out of your work. It's about going for a *high-quality* selling experience.

Finally, this book is part of my personal crusade to get the word out that selling is not about charisma, personality, or a set of inherited traits that can be found only in the chromosomes. Effective selling comes from the application of a set of skills and behaviors anyone can learn. And I mean *anyone*. Properly applied, these skills will serve you well in whatever work you do and in every aspect of your life.

The bottom line in today's workplace is simply this: There is no such thing as job security. In his autobiography, *Odyssey*, John Sculley, former chairman of Apple Computer, wrote about this situation. He recalled telling his own employees that Apple could not promise jobs for life, but (to paraphrase) whether you are here for six weeks, or six months, or three years, or fifteen years, we can and do promise you an exciting learning experience that will make you better and more valuable in the job market than you were when you walked in the door.

Tom Peters, in an article he wrote for *Working Woman*, said, "The only security in a world where job security is gone is that your skills are better and your network richer at the end of this year than they were at the beginning. Your ability to improve your skill base and make yourself more marketable, whether you are a teamster or a neurosurgeon, is the only thing you've got."

In an environment where the average American will have seven different careers in his or her lifetime, what skills will you need next? Nobody can say. But I will say this: Sales skills are no longer optional.

Nothing happens until something is sold.

ANONYMOUS

Mama, Don't Let Your Babies Grow Up to Be Salespeople

A s I said in the Introduction, in one way or another, we're all in sales. I know, I know: *You're* not in sales. You're a district manager, or a human resources counselor, or an engineer. You're a doctor or a lawyer. You're a butcher, a baker, a candlestick maker. But not a *sales*person. Oh, *no!*

And yet, don't you sometimes find yourself helping someone—oh, say, a *customer*—fill some need or other? Don't you occasionally talk about your service or product to people who might—wild guess here—*buy* it?

What about when you went looking for a job? Didn't you have to contact complete strangers and persuade them to let you come into their offices and take up their valuable time with a presentation you hoped would convince them to give you money for your services? And when you got that job, didn't you then have to service your new "account" so your "customer" would continue to pay your weekly "premiums"? And if you wanted those weekly payments to increase by way of a promotion or a raise, didn't you have to provide your employer with new or better service than your "competitors"—the other employees?

Let's say your name tag reads "receptionist." Can you really ignore the profound impact your treatment of callers and visitors can have on their decisions about whether to continue doing business with your company? If they do stay with you, won't that translate into more *sales?* And aren't you partly responsible for those increased or at least continued sales?

What if your official title is "installer"? Won't being positive, knowledgeable, and helpful influence customers to call again? Won't those calls lead to more invoices? More—you got it—*sales?*

And you cashiers out there! Isn't it true that by sheer dint of ill will, you can cut sharply into your store's profits? Conversely, won't courtesy and genuine concern for the needs of your customers improve profits? Of course they will!

Now, if all of that isn't *selling,* I'm a platypus.

All sarcasm aside (for now), the point I'm trying to make here is this: If you look carefully and honestly at the dynamics of the vast majority of your professional interactions (and a heck of a lot of your personal ones), you're going to find that you are, in fact, involved quite intimately with a very specific process called "selling."

The Selling Engine

We live in a capitalist country, and selling is the high-octane fuel that makes the engine of our economy run. It's been said that in America selling isn't really a profession; it's *the* profession. And I believe mastering the skills of that profession is a matter of survival.

Even those in the so-called traditional professions, who may find it difficult to think of their patients, students, or clients as customers, cannot escape this fact. Maybe that's why so many professional schools have begun to include business and management classes in their curricula. "Financial issues for physicians" seminars seem to be cropping up everywhere, teaching neophyte healers to think of their patients as consumers of health care services with lots of options and no particular loyalty to any one provider. Respected attorneys are employing advertising and marketing strategies that would have branded them as ambulance chasers only a few years ago. Dentists are joining referral services to drum up new business. They've all discovered that, in addition to a license, they need at least a smattering of the human interface skills required to function effectively in this dynamic and unforgiving economy.

Even those back-room types who seem to be the least likely of all to come face to face with an actual customer (rocket scientists, software engineers, hard-core academics) cannot escape. The environment in which we all live and work makes it inevitable that they will find themselves in sales situations, even if they don't recognize them as such. Let me give you an example:

A few years ago, I met with a group of dusty but earnest university professors who wanted me to help them figure out

Professionals Sell

A chiropractor I know is a perfect example of a professional who not only understands that there is a sales component to his business but also embraces the notion, to the great benefit of his customers and his practice. Jerry started out very small with a one-man operation, but because he listened to his customers and wasn't afraid to respond to their needs as a sales professional would, his

why enrollment in a certain department of their school was declining. We sat down together at a conference table, they eyed me suspiciously, and I asked them a question that turned out to be something of a bomb. I said, "What do you sell here?"

"What do we sell?" they asked, more or less together. "We don't sell anything! We're here in the pursuit of knowledge!"

"Okay," I said, "how do you feel about pursuing that knowledge without a paycheck?"

"They can't get rid of us. We have tenure!"

"If you've got no students," I said, "you've got no tenure."

That quieted them down to a low grumble.

What the professors hadn't yet realized was that their students—really, their customers—had quite a few educational options from which to choose. They could go to competing universities. They could get their education via correspondence study or videotapes. They could go to school in Mexico or the Philippines for a quarter of the cost. Or they could just not go at all.

practice grew quickly to a six-person operation. He consistently built complementary services into his business, hiring a masseuse as soon as he could afford to, and later adding a physical therapist to his staff. He not only provided complementary services for the good of his patients; he also built a thriving practice that is still growing. And as far as his very satisfied customers are concerned, he is still a professional.

More important, these professors had failed to grasp the important role they played in the *selling* process.

"Let's say I'm interested in pursuing the profession this program prepares me for," I said, shamelessly ending my sentence with a preposition. "Describe it to me."

In a nutshell, their responses went something like this: "Well, it's a very long road, it's very difficult, and at the end of it you might not be able to get a job. If you do get a job, the opportunities for promotion are very few and far between. Oh, and there is a lot of discrimination against women in this profession."

Eeew! Why in heaven's name would anyone spend thousands of dollars and years of their lives in a program like that?

Without realizing it, these well-intentioned folks had been sabotaging their own program. While I certainly would never advise them to lie to potential students about the downside of any profession, their dreary description was anything but the complete picture. They left out the fact that it is a dynamic field

You're Selling—Even If You Don't Realize It

A few years ago I was using my local school district as an example of bad customer service. I told seminar attendees how I had tried to get some information about district boundaries and ended up going to five different offices where five different people couldn't help me. After hours of waiting and hassles, I ended up with no information at all.

When the local superintendent of schools heard about my experience, she called me up, apologized, and offered not only to get me the maps I had wanted but also

in which you learn every day and in which a person could truly help others. They also failed to mention that they all thought it was the most satisfying and meaningful work in the world.

Now, *that's* a program the right student would buy.

My professors were very smart guys, but I had to give them an F in Selling 101. Until that meeting, it hadn't sunk in that they needed to develop some sales savvy if they wanted to keep their jobs. As it turned out, they were fast studies. They began to pay attention to things like class times, student parking, their own descriptions of the work, and classroom amenities. With a simple change in attitude, enrollment grew over the next few years, and the department began to flourish.

That's just one example of how nonsales types who take the time to pay attention to sales fundamentals can make a difference. I could give you many more. (And I will, if you keep reading.)

to personally deliver the maps to each department so that this would never happen again.

She didn't blame or make excuses. She took the responsibility herself for fixing the problem and for taking care of me, the customer. This was relationship selling at its best, though I doubt the superintendent thought of her actions that way. She didn't just *say* she would make the call; she didn't *mean* to make the call; she *made the call*. She got me on the horn, listened to my problems, and made things right.

I still talk about the school district in my seminars, but now I use it as the *good* example.

Of course, I can tell this isn't going over with some of you. I can read it in your faces (well, I could if I could see them). That's all well and good, you're thinking, but the truth is, I really don't care about this company's bottom line. Heck, they sure don't care about me! Just look at last year's layoff statistics. I don't care how many pamphlets they publish telling us we're a family. I could be out on the street at any time!

Fair enough. *And all the more reason to hone your sales skills!* In today's volatile workplace, sales skills are the most transferable. If you find yourself out on the pavement fighting for scarce jobs, you will always be welcome in some sales department.

But you don't need an actual sales job to get value from these skills. You will use them in your job search and then later in your new position. And having sales fundamentals firmly under your belt may be the closest thing you will ever get to job security. Mastery of ethical selling techniques will make you a more effective and thus more valuable employee. Sales, after all, is about understanding people, communication, and a unique kind of teamwork. Good salespeople are good listeners, creative problem solvers, and dynamic self-starters. If you were an employer, wouldn't you keep a person with those characteristics as long as you could? In fact, wouldn't you promote that person?

Selling Is As Selling Does

What is selling? At its highest level—the one for which we're shooting here—it's the process of recognizing and satisfying a need in order to create and keep customers. It's about being observant, caring, and respectful. It's about listening in a certain way. And it's about solving problems.

It is *not* about making a quota, moving the "merch," or scamming suckers. Although these things can happen when you sell (except for scamming—and the only sucker in *that* equation is the scammer), the most effective salespeople I've known seemed to view these things almost as by-products of the interaction. Sure, if you're a sales guy or gal, you gotta make sales, but the truly Olympic performers never seem focused on moving the merch. They're awake, alive, and on purpose. Their perspectives are long term, and their priorities involve meeting the customers' needs first. They believe their interests and the interests of their customers are inextricably linked. They are people who want to look back on a life of accomplishments, not just a succession of paychecks. In the words of master salesman Zig Ziglar, "They see themselves getting what they want by making sure enough other people get what *they* want."

Unfortunately, much of what passes for sales training nowadays amounts to nothing more than mindless bullying. Too many managers are of the get-out-there-and-make-it-happen-and-no-excuses school. Too many salespeople are taught to keep their eyes exclusively on their quotas and the short-term bottom line. (If this is news to you, stop by your local video store and rent *Glengarry Glenn Ross,* and you'll see a grim example of what I'm talking about.)

With 70 percent of the salespeople in this country mistrained and/or maltrained, is there any wonder the profession of selling has acquired such a bad name?

The preponderance of bad sales training notwithstanding, there's a lot to be learned from the other 30 percent. Truly effective salespeople are a happy, fulfilled, and genuinely magnetic bunch. They've mastered an important set of skills, and they use those skills well and with integrity. They are high-quality people who enjoy their work and take pride in their profession. And they are paid very well for what they do.

We can all learn a lot from the 30 percenters. And what we learn we can apply to everyday situations. These "everyday selling skills" equip us to recognize and to respond appropriately to a variety of situations and to benefit from our efforts. They equip us to be *situational*—knowing when to sell, when to listen, and when to shut up and move on.

Speaking of which . . .

CHAPTER

2

The royal road to a man's heart is to talk to him about the things he treasures most.

THEODORE ROOSEVELT

Your Selling Aptitude
A Short Quiz

Whenever I start something new, whether it's a business project, a class, an exercise program, or whatever, I usually take a minute to "rank" myself at the beginning. It's not a big deal and doesn't take long, but it's become a very useful habit. When I'm trying to lose weight, like most people, I step on a scale the morning of the first day. When I started my walking program, I jotted down in my Daytimer how far I walked on my first outing as well as how I felt when I finished. Each time I take on a new computer program, I notice how uncomfortable and lost I am when I start working with it, and I make a note each time I master a new procedure.

Before you read further, I think it would be a good idea to take a minute to assess your current sales skills. To help you do that, I've put together a short true/false quiz. It'll not only measure your sales acumen but also stick a thermometer into your attitude about the whole process. It's not a big deal, it won't take long, and it'll give you something to check yourself against later on.

Ready? Here goes. Identify the following statements as either true or false:

1. Everyone is selling something.

2. Selling is a profession characterized by a set of skills and behaviors with a highly quantifiable outcome.

3. Selling "on purpose" means the other party's satisfaction is as important to you as your own.

4. Most parents hope that their children will grow up to be salespeople.

5. It is possible to sell people something they do not want.

6. The most successful salespeople are great talkers, have a huge inventory of jokes (some repeatable for mixed company), and are *tall*.

7. The best selling occurs when a relationship is established between the salesperson and the customer.

8. Professional and technical people do not need to sell their services.

9. The hardest part of any job is the sales function.

10. Selling is an inherent skill; either you have it or you don't.

11. If a product or service is good enough, it will sell itself.

12. Good salespeople are not bothered by rejection.

13. The 80/20 rule means that 20 percent of customers generate 80 percent of sales, so only this 20 percent should get first-class treatment.

14. Selling can be stressless, satisfying, and financially rewarding.

15. There are some jobs that have no selling aspect to them.

16. The difference between a salesperson and a clerk is the ability to overcome objections.

17. Salespeople fight a constant battle to remain motivated.

18. Objections can be overcome by unrelenting pressure, facts, statistics, and testimonials.

19. Creating a selling "approach" is manipulative.

20. Customers can only be sold the difference between what they have and what they want.

Okay, the truth or falsehood of the above statements aren't eternal verities, but this book does have a point of view. Here's what I think about all this:

1. *True.* Throughout this book I will attempt to inform, persuade, and *sell* you on the astonishing value of adopting a positive selling mentality. Wherever you currently find yourself on the management food chain, exhibiting professional selling behavior will enhance your opportunities for advancement and job satisfaction.

2. *True.* Unfortunately, many people might consider this a trick question because of my use of the word "profession." It is, however, my very firm belief that selling *is* a profession— maybe *the* profession. Classical definitions aside, salespeople are as essential to our mutual survival as doctors, lawyers, and teachers. Without them and what they do, there simply is no economy.

3. *True*. The fundamental premise of this book is that selling is not about flimflam or smooth talk. Salespeople who create and keep customers are the ones who make sure those customers' needs are met, over and over again.

4. *False*. What? Are you kidding? Whenever I ask seminar participants which ones would be delighted to learn their children had decided to go into sales, I get looks of pure horror. And yet, not only do top salespeople have the highest income potential, but also many report being more fulfilled and satisfied than the CEOs and company presidents who supposedly direct their work. Who could want more for their kids?

5. *True*. I probably caught you on this one. The trick word here is "want." When you think about it, much of the American economy is based on selling people things they want but don't really need. I mean, does anyone really *need* a Lexus? Couldn't we all wear brand X jeans as well as Guess? Effective selling is about creating desire in the customer for what we provide or do.

6. *False*. Many highly effective salespeople are quiet, deliberative—and *short*! Good selling skills and behaviors are based on listening and responding to the customer. Many times, the highly voluble sales approach drowns out the customers' requests and looks like a high-pressure sales blitzkrieg.

7. *True*. One of the biggest payoffs of effective selling is the opportunity to establish an ongoing relationship with customers. This isn't a wham-bam-thank-you-ma'am approach. Long-term sales success comes from repeat business; repeat business grows out of effective relationships.

8. *False*. In today's churning business climate, *everybody* needs to sell! And remember, I contend that selling can be effortless, professional, and done with integrity. The act of selling need not compromise any technical or professional standards.

9. *False.* Individuals who develop a "selling-on-purpose" attitude find the sales function to be not only one of the easiest parts of their jobs but often the most pleasurable as well. There's nothing like creating a satisfied customer.

10. *False, false, false!* Selling is a *learned* skill. No one is a born salesman, and no two salespeople do it the same way. If you come away from this book with only one message, I hope it's this one.

11. *False.* I continue to run into people who believe that their products or services are so doggone wonderful all they really need to do is get the word out and flocks of salivating customers will hurtle themselves at the showroom window with their wallets outstretched. Of course, they've forgotten a little American concept called "competition." There's always someone else out there offering a product or service close enough to yours from the customers' point of view to get their attention—and their business.

12. *False.* The tricky phrase here is "not bothered." In sales, rejection is inevitable, and sales pros know it, but that doesn't mean it doesn't hurt. But the pros also know how to separate rejection of their product or service from rejection of themselves personally. It's a vital skill that allows them to regenerate the enthusiasm they need to go on to the next prospect.

13. *False.* The question does state accurately the tried-and-true selling maxim, but sales professionals give first-class treatment to every customer. Top salespeople are in the business of creating and keeping customers. Effective selling can "convert" some of that 80 percent, and that's the name of the game.

14. *True.* One of the most satisfying aspects of truly effective selling is the beautiful harvest of repeat business and the effortless flow of new business from excellent word of mouth from satisfied customers.

15. *False.* Having worked my way through college in a variety of clerical jobs that are as far down the career chain as you can get, I can report from firsthand experience that every job, from pounding a keyboard eight hours a day in a title company to juggling 120 calls per hour on a switchboard, has a selling aspect. The energy expended to find out not just about the immediate "job" but also about the organization and the people in it constitutes selling. (If more data-entry people and receptionists had sales training, they would feel more qualified and empowered to represent their jobs and their companies with pride.)

16. *True, true, true!* So many workers fall into what I call the *sales clerk syndrome*. They stock shelves and ring up sales on the cash register, and it never occurs to them that they have any responsibility to interact with real live customers, let alone respond to objections. Salespeople welcome objections. It gives them an opportunity to demonstrate their expertise and discover whether their product or service actually solves the customer's problem.

17. *True.* In my opinion, *everybody* fights a constant battle to remain motivated. (Except, of course, for those who have chosen the whine-and-make-excuses strategy.) We're all under pressure nowadays to perform, to keep up with changing customer needs, and to stay abreast of new products and services. A high level of motivation is essential to success in any endeavor.

18. *True.* However, unrelenting pressure, facts, statistics, and testimonials are not the most *effective* means for overcoming objections.

19. *False.* Creating an effective selling approach is essential to sales success. Understanding that it's not always what you say but how you say it is *not* manipulative. It's accepting and utilizing a fundamental tenet of communication.

20. *True.* The most effective salespeople let go of their need to sell a particular product or service and concentrate on selling what their customers want to buy. It's the best way I know to make the selling practically effortless.

The secret of success is constancy to purpose.

BENJAMIN DISRAELI

Selling 101 for Nonsalespeople

This book is not intended to address sales in the traditional sense. In these pages we'll look at the concepts and principles of good, effective salesmanship in other contexts outside the usual sales environment. But in the end, we're still talking about *selling*, and to understand that complex subject we must consult traditional sources.

As I pointed out in Chapter 1, there's a lot to be learned about selling from the most effective practitioners in the field. Over the years, it's been my privilege to work with many well-established top performers and many rising stars. Each is an individual with his or her own strengths, style, and personality.

But without exception, all of these highly effective professionals learned, practiced, and honed the same fundamental sales skills.

In this chapter we'll go over those fundamental skills. I know this sounds a lot like actual *sales stuff* (gasp!), but I swear these principles are absolutely crucial. In fact, the rest of the book just wouldn't make sense without them.

Think of this chapter as your selling primer. Take the time to absorb what follows, and I guarantee you won't regret it.

The Characteristics of Successful Salespeople

In my experience, all truly effective salespeople have certain things in common, certain traits or characteristics they have developed within themselves that serve them in their work. I'm not talking about assets they may have been born with—physical attractiveness, for example, or that mythical sales gene that keeps so many of us from bothering to try to learn this stuff. I'm talking about decisions they made about how to conduct themselves—decisions the rest of us can make, too.

Self-Starters

I believe the most important characteristic of a successful salesperson—most successful *people*, for that matter—is their ability to get up and at 'em on their own. I have never met a successful salesperson who was not a self-starter. Self-starters don't look elsewhere for motivation. They take for granted that they are going to set their own goals, and they're not looking for a leader to tell them what to do with their lives. They take responsibility for themselves and their work. They get up, get going, and make sure they have the knowledge and the equipment they need to do the best job of which they are capable.

The ability to be a self-starter is obviously crucial in other pursuits as well. What parent worthy of the title waits around for someone else to tell him how to raise his children? What supervisor worth her salt lets others determine her agenda? What job seeker with any hope of finding employment waits for employers to call him?

Effective salespeople are the ones who get up and act on their own. They're not necessarily born that way, but they have discovered that it's a much more effective way to live.

Persistence

Nearly as important as the ability to act on your own is the capacity to hang in there. Thomas Edison, arguably the world's greatest inventor, recorded *25,000 failures* in his attempt to invent the storage battery. "Those were not failures," he said when interviewed. "I just learned 25,000 ways *not* to make a storage battery." Babe Ruth, the greatest hitter in the history of baseball with 714 home runs in his career, *struck out 1,330 times.* Both men achieved what they did because they *persisted.*

To paraphrase former President Dwight D. Eisenhower, success is not about genius or effort; it's about *persistence.* Nothing succeeds like a stubborn unwillingness to give up. It's certainly true that there are times in all our lives when we should let go, when it's time to leave a job or replace an unrealistic expectation with a more realistic goal, but frankly, that's not usually the problem. What I find most often in my consulting practice are capable people who just won't stick with their goals/relationships/projects/whatever long enough to find out whether they would have worked out or not. This is especially true in sales. That's why the trait of persistence is so obvious in successful salespeople.

To quote Jimmy Stewart in that great old western *Destry Rides Again,* "You gotta make like a postage stamp and stick to something long enough to get somewhere."

A Love of People

One of the most compelling qualities of the successful salespeople I've known is their genuine affection for people. All people. In general. They like meeting new ones and visiting old friends. They're not put off by different races or cultures. They meet even language barriers with equanimity and patient warmth. These qualities make such people positively *magnetic.*

What's more, they *act* like they like people. In other words, everyone knows they like them, because they show it in myriad ways. It's not a secret that we all find out at the reading of the will: "Yeah, I couldn't believe it. He left me his time-share in *Cancun.* Said I was his best friend. I didn't even know the guy knew my last name."

Side note: It's ironic to me that so many of the folks I meet in my work who introduce themselves as "people persons" turn out to have nothing but contempt for their fellow humans. What they really mean is they like people who are like them or who agree with them. That means, of course, they *don't* like most people.

High Energy

The most energetic people I know are salespeople, bar none. They get themselves up, they get themselves going, and they *keep themselves going.* They realize that bodies in motion tend to stay in motion. They also realize that if they're going to make a sale, they've got to be excited about the product or service. And they take responsibility for generating that excitement within themselves.

Energy was the main issue for one of my favorite clients. A very smart, capable man, Ed had been in business for himself for about five years. He was a wonderful guy, a former book-keeper who had been selling bookkeeping services on his own with a certain respectable success.

But Ed was having trouble growing his business to any significant degree. All of his current clients were very happy with him and thought of him as a highly competent professional who delivered the goods. Yet he couldn't seem to generate much new business

I decided to go on a few sales calls with Ed, sort of a fishing trip, to see if I could hook into his problem. I got a bite on our first call.

A quiet man by nature, Ed was a wonderful listener, and listening is a vital skill for effective sales (a subject on which I'll expand later). But Ed's was one of the rare cases of taking this very important skill too far. He was so quiet, so reluctant to assert himself, so tentative, he came off like a guy who didn't believe in his service or himself. It sometimes took him twenty minutes to choke out his presentation. He sucked so much energy out of the room, it was all the prospect and I could do to stay awake!

When I pointed this situation out to him, he was terrifically flexible about it (one of the reasons he's one of my favorites). "I like to project calmness," he told me, "but if I'm so calm I'm putting people to sleep, I'd better rethink that strategy."

It turns out Ed is a competitive marathoner. He told me how he'd "get himself up" for a race. I suggested he adapt his prerace ritual, which included focusing on his strengths (features) and visualizing his success (seeing the sale), to a pre-presentation warm-up. He liked that idea and felt sure he could make the adjustment.

Ed managed to ignite a spark that heated up the energy in his presentations—with almost immediate results. In less than a year, he doubled his business.

Proactivity

Effective salespeople take charge of their lives and live in a world they believe they create—mostly. None of us can do much about natural disasters, accidents, and certain diseases. I'm not selling an illusion of ultimate control here. I am saying there are often too many things in our lives that we neglect until the universe comes crashing down on us. If we're overweight and out of shape, we can exercise and eat less today or have a heart attack tomorrow. If we smoke, we can get help and quit today or have lung cancer tomorrow. If we're chronically late now, we can make a conscious effort to change that habit or look like an unprofessional flake for the rest of our careers. If we need an advanced degree to move ahead in our chosen profession, we can make the sacrifices, do the work, and get that degree, or we can stagnate, grow bitter, and retire on the job.

Proactivity is about *acting* instead of *reacting*. Proactive people don't wait for the world to happen to them. They take the responsibility for themselves. They strive to become *the* dynamic force in their own lives.

One very good example of a proactive person is Randy, a flooring contractor I worked with a few years ago. Randy began to notice the effect the hard manual labor he had done nearly every day of his life since he was sixteen was beginning to have on his knees. All those hours of crawling around on rooftops and down on his knees laying carpet and tile had begun to take their toll. He wasn't in agony yet, but he could see that the ache wasn't going to go away. So he consulted a doctor and learned that he would probably need surgery in a few years and eventually would indeed have to find another line of work.

Nobody made Randy call his doctor. He could just as easily have ignored the problem until he was unable to work, then scrambled desperately for something else. (I'll bet you can name at least five people in your life who are ignoring equally critical issues in their lives.) Instead, he called his doctor and learned the truth. Then he called me, and we began putting together a career-change strategy.

Long before his knees would have given out, Randy quit construction work and began managing the contractor supply department of a major hardware chain. He felt comfortable in the environment, he liked the people for whom and with he worked, and he had expert product knowledge. Within five years he was moving up the management ladder and heading for a corner office.

Oh, and because he left his former trade early enough, his knees made a full recovery.

Consultants

The best salespeople see themselves as consultants. They realize that nothing is forever, that they are, in fact, disposable. This sounds bad, but this point of view gives them certain advantages. For one, they have the luxury of being able to see a bigger picture. And in a way, they're freer to focus 100 percent of their attention on what the other person is asking. Good consultants respond to what their clients want, ask a lot of questions, then diagnose—and prepare to solve—problems.

Too Much of a Good Thing

Margaret is a CPA in her early thirties with a wall of degrees and certificates—and a great big pink slip. She had been working as a professional accountant for several years when she decided she would make more money and find more opportunity as a stockbroker. So she went to school and earned the necessary certifications and found a job as a stockbroker. But then she decided she should

Lifelong Learners

The most effective salespeople are always learning—about new products, new people, and the world around them. They are excited when opportunities to learn come along, and they make the most of them. In fact, learning is a habit with them.

This does not mean staying on a path of constant self-improvement out of insecurity or a belief that you're not good enough. The quality I'm talking about here is one of honest curiosity and a love of the ever-changing material world. These people not only embrace change but also prepare themselves for it. They are not only curious but also unafraid to get in there and *learn new things.* They want to understand more about complex financial matters, so they take a class at a junior college. One of their clients wants to send them an e-mail, so they get the neighbor's ten-year-old to teach them about the Internet. New technologies, new markets, new customers: none of it ever throws them, because they see it all as an opportunity to *learn.*

become a certified financial planner. So she went to school for that. Unfortunately, while she was chasing after more and better credentials, she failed to sell any stock, so she lost her job.

Especially nowadays, continuing education is vital to your success. But don't make a career out of it. Ultimately, it's not just what you know, it's what people want to buy from you.

Again, it's a choice they make. Frankly, it's a choice we had all better think about very seriously. Whatever you may think about all this sales stuff, this quality is one I believe with all my heart we must all adopt. And the sooner, the better. (More on this later.)

Flexibility

Sure, it's important to be able to touch your toes, but what I'm talking about here is *mental* and *emotional* flexibility. Effective salespeople can go with the flow, adapt to change, shift their expectations, and let go of concepts that no longer serve them.

Being flexible is also about being *fluid*. Effective salespeople know that the manual won't have the answer for every question that comes up or a strategy for dealing with every individual customer. They use the rules when they are appropriate, but they are awake to the specifics of the moment. And they are not shackled by the need to force a particular situation into a predetermined box. They can move with the music, so to speak, even when the tempo changes.

In terms of management flexibility, Nordstrom clothing stores are legendary. In lieu of providing their sales associates with lists of dos and don'ts, Nordstrom managers empower their employees, telling them simply to use their best judgment in every situation. Hire good people, this management philosophy says, and let them follow their instincts.

Not Afraid to Make Money

You'd be surprised what an issue this is for some people—and what an impediment to personal effectiveness. Lots of people have said to me, "Brig, the money just doesn't matter to me." Uh-huh. I'm sorry, but I don't buy it. Sure, we all do things for the sheer love of the challenge or the activity itself, but it's still about *gain*, which is money without the dead presidents.

Some people just can't seem to allow themselves to let financial gain be part of their conscious motivation. I agree that it's important to love your work, but come on, folks, we all want and deserve to be paid for our efforts. (I think a little bit of shame may come into this picture somewhere, but I'll leave discussions of our inner child to others.)

Even when we're not really doing it for the money, aren't we doing it for things like recognition, the gratitude of others, personal fulfillment, being true to ourselves, or plain old fun? If we don't know what we hope to gain from our efforts, how will we know whether the effort was worth it?

We have to let ourselves in on what our reasons are for taking on the challenges we choose in this life. We don't have to announce them to the world, but our motivations cannot be a secret to *us!* If we don't know why we're doing something, we won't have a clear intention, and that can sidetrack the best of us.

The best salespeople I know are highly motivated by material gain. More important, they are not ashamed of that fact. Money, for them, is the scorecard. And they're playing the game to win.

Quality Minded

This, of course, goes against every sales guy stereotype, but my experience with highly effective salespeople convinces me that these folks are very concerned about the quality of the products or services they sell. One sales rep I know once explained it to me this way: "I sell gold, my name gets associated with gold. I sell garbage, my name gets associated with garbage. Which would you want?"

The quality-mindedness of highly effective salespeople shows up in other areas, too. It's the little things, mostly. That extra effort; putting the presentation in a nice spiral-bound folder. It's not complicated, expensive, or time-consuming, but it says, "I'm proud of my work, and I want to give it my best shot." There are millions of shortcuts, but that little extra effort makes a huge difference.

Before the Sale

Along with cultivating the characteristics I've listed here, the best salespeople also take the time to prepare themselves *before* they meet with a potential customer. They may look like they're winging it, but that's just a by-product of careful preparation. I'm not talking about memorizing canned scripts, which the best people never do. I'm talking about the kind of physical and mental planning you find among top athletes and actors.

Many report going through a kind of preflight checklist: Appearance appropriate? Check. Product knowledge complete? Check. Attitude adjusted? Check. How did you like it last time? Did it work out for you? It makes customers crazy when salespeople start from zero, so scan your memory banks and ask them about what you sold them last time. How did that commercial work for you, Mr. Jones? The less effective salespeople don't ask, because they really don't want to know.

This is an important part of the sales process. It's about building confidence and getting rid of personal impediments. If I know I look good, if I'm sure I can handle any questions thrown at me (or I know where to get the answers I don't have), and if I'm open and interested in whomever I might meet—I'm *ready*.

Let's take a closer look at these three prep-check items.

Appearance

The first item on our checklist seems obvious, but it is ignored far too often. This isn't about looking "good"; it's about looking *appropriate*. It's about taking the time to present yourself in a way that won't prevent others from connecting with you. It's about having your hair combed and your pants pressed. It's about being *clean*. And increasingly, it's about not smoking.

This definitely isn't brain surgery, and it should be fairly easy to figure out, but appearance can become a very big deal if neglected. In his book *How to Make Big Money Selling*, Joe Gandolfo talks about it this way:

Because customers have different values and personal standards, some employers encourage their salespeople to communicate a safe or conservative image. Employers in some
environments, such as restaurants, require uniforms. Others,
such as sophisticated fashion stores, ask their salespeople to
adhere to dress codes. When accepting a new position it's a
good idea to discuss the matter of grooming and image
before reporting for work.

The most effective salespeople I know go about this business of dealing with their appearance by simply striving to fit
into or exceed the environment into which they put themselves.
They put on the "costume" that's appropriate to the stage. They
wear makeup and pantyhose when that's appropriate (this usually applies to women). They learn how to properly knot a necktie when that's important. And if they're working in an art
gallery, they stay away from Brooks Brothers.

This should be easy, not something we stumble over, yet a
lot of people resent this notion. They say, "My appearance
should not be an issue. That's superficial. It's what's inside that
counts."

Okay, you can't judge a book by its cover. But guess what:
That's exactly what people do. Literally and figuratively. That's
why publishers spend so much money on a great cover design.
The content may be what counts in the end, but in the beginning of the relationship, if the cover doesn't attract the reader,
she may never open the book in the first place. Would you
really walk into a job interview with a mohawk hairdo, a torn T-
shirt, safety pins for earrings, and big, black Doc Marten com-
bat boots? Four-inch fingernails painted talon red are cool,
sure, but aren't they also distracting as hell? And would you

really pick your kids up from school in hair curlers and a bathrobe?

Zig Zigler, the godfather of modern sales technique, writes about going into a restaurant and being served by a guy with tattoos on his forearms, earrings, and a pierced nose. "I went to war, and I fought for the right for that person to do that," he says, "but I would never hire him. I have that right, too."

Maybe appearance shouldn't matter, but what's true here? The truth is there's too much competition out there to let eccentric or inappropriate clothing or grooming distract a potential buyer from what you're selling. The question to ask yourself is whether you, by your choices in this area, are limiting your options.

Product Knowledge

I'm always giving lectures about how you can't know too much about your product or service, your customers, and your market. Yet this part of the selling process often gets short shrift.

How can you sell something you don't know thoroughly? When top salespeople sit down to talk with a client, they know what they're talking about. Period. They've done their homework, they've used the product or service, and they can speak with confidence gained from experience. They know that knowing as much as you can about your product—especially experiencing it yourself when that's possible—makes selling *effortless*.

For me, product knowledge—particularly personal experience—is the acid test. If I'm dealing with a salesperson who doesn't know his stuff, I'm immediately turned off. Before I buy, I always ask whether the salesperson uses the product himself. There's only one answer to that question: "Yes, and I love it!" Anything else, and I'm outta there.

The bottom line: Before you can sell it effectively, you gotta know what you're selling.

Attitude

Whether you know it or not, your attitude shows. That may sound like a bumper sticker, but it's important enough that it should have been carved in granite with a fiery finger from above. It's one of those little things that others know about you that you don't know yourself. And it's one of the things of which top sales pros are acutely aware.

Whatever you're doing, it's never enough to show up and go through the motions. You have to be awake to what you're thinking and feeling, or your attitude is going to sabotage your efforts. You may be smiling, shaking hands, and cracking jokes, but your facial expressions and body language give you away. If what's under that smile is something like, "I'll bet she won't buy this," or "They just raised the price on this piece of crap, but I guess I'll show it to them anyway," you might as well have stayed in bed.

This is a good place to point out the high cost of intolerance. I've watched salespeople approaching minority customers with "this is a waste of time because *they* can't afford this" written all over their faces. People, especially minorities, are very sensitive to nonverbal clues. Believe me, the color of a customer's skin is a lousy indicator of how much they're willing and able to spend. But the color of your attitude toward them could cost you some serious green.

Speaking of bumper stickers, here are two of my favorites: "Your actions are speaking so loudly, I can't hear your words" and "People may not believe what you say, but they'll always believe what you do."

I think those were written by salespeople.

Needs Determination

Once a seasoned pro is in the sales situation, he or she starts by determining the needs of the potential buyer. Average to mediocre salespeople spend their time worrying about what they want to sell; great salespeople pay attention to what the customer wants to buy.

Understanding buying motives is crucial to successful selling. It's never what you want to sell; it's always what they want to buy. This is true in nonsales applications, too. If, for example, you're applying for a job in a company's engineering department, you might start by asking what they're looking for.

"Well," they might say, "we're looking specifically for an engineer who has experience in the infrastructure of bridge spans. What's your experience?"

"I have experience in the infrastructure of bridge spans."

See how it works?

There are basically five reasons people buy anything (call them "buying motives"): pleasure, economy, pride, utility, and protection. This can be about the product, but more often than not it's about the salesperson.

Pleasure

This is the number-one buying motive in our culture. Not only are we interested in acquiring products and services that give us pleasure, but also we want the buying experience itself to be pleasurable.

Also, we like being around people who are pleasant, easy to get along with, and productive—people who contribute to the pleasure of that buying experience. Sales pros know this; the best ones know you can't make it too easy.

Economy

People buy if it looks like a good deal. If I think I can hire you for less than the other guy, all other things being equal, I'll probably do it. It's a simple, direct motive. That's why people clip coupons and comparison shop.

But remember, *price* and *cost* are very different concepts. If your price is more than they expected, but you present it with confidence and an honest belief that you're worth it, they might buy you anyway. We all like to get a deal, but we also like to get our money's worth. Economy, in this context, is about value. It's not always how much we spend; sometimes it's what we perceive a particular product or service to be worth.

Pride

There's nothing like a brand name. Oh, sure, people buy generic goods all the time, but if a label didn't matter, every box on the shelf would be black and white, and Bufferin, Tide, and Häagen-Dazs would be out of business. The truth is, people like to own quality stuff. Mont Blanc, Lexus, and Harvard hold a definite power over Bic, Hyundai, and Central Junior College. Name-brand products communicate something about the buyer, and it's a strong buying motive.

I think I only really understood this buying motive after I earned my second graduate degree from a prestigious university (Pepperdine). At first I just dismissed the idea that my degree would make a difference, which many of us do. But then I realized that people perceived my worth to be higher. And by golly, I finally decided to charge them more for me.

Utility

A big reason we buy goods and services is that we need them. My car breaks down, so I'm highly motivated to seek out the services of a mechanic. My company is transferring me to Stuttgart, so I'm highly motivated to seek the services of a German language instructor. I've got a problem, and your goods or services are going to solve that problem. Where's my checkbook?

Many not-so-effective salespeople could shorten the sales process considerably by paying attention to this buying motive. You don't have to go on and on about what a wonderful day care provider you are when the fact of the matter is that the buyer has made twenty unsuccessful phone calls and you're the only one who takes infants. They live close to you, they can afford you, and you've got what they want. Now shut up.

Conversely, if I'm trying to sell to someone who's buying for utility, and I'm a wonderful child care provider, but they don't have any kids, I'm clearly wasting my time. (Sounds silly, but I've seen that very example.)

Protection

Insurance is sold with this buying motive; so are higher quality products and extra features. We buy them so we won't have problems down the road. This motive comes from a desire to avoid trouble.

One of my clients provides a payroll service that is drawing more and more clients because of the huge government fines and penalties for mistakes. He does the payroll accurately, and he takes the heat when there's an audit.

People sometimes say to me, "Brig, I know how important the buying motive is, but sometimes it's impossible to get people to tell you why they might want to buy."

I say that the harder it is to get it out of them, the more likely it's a buying motive like pleasure or pride, the softer ones.

This can be especially frustrating during a job search. The company says it's hiring; it puts an ad in the paper listing the qualifications it's seeking. You fit the ad like a glove, but they hem and haw during the interview and say they'll give you a call. It turns out what they really wanted was someone with a lot of energy to fire up the research-and-development team. Of course, they didn't *say* that in the ad or the interview.

So, the more ambiguous the buyer's motives seem, the less likely the issue is price. When the buyer's motives elude you, look to qualitative issues. For the job seeker in the above example, he might try saying things like, "I can really get along with people," "I'm really involved in the community," or "I enjoy the work I do with the Boy Scouts." Watch their reactions, and you might be able to ferret out what they're after. (Of course, they may not know themselves, which makes things all the harder.)

Objections

Overcoming objections is a key skill of highly effective salespeople. The first step is learning not to be afraid of objections. When the very best salespeople talk about objections in selling, they . . . well . . . they *like* them. A lot. No kidding. Objections are actually positive contributions to the selling process. The customer is still talking with us. We're still being given useful information. And we're still talking about the transaction itself. The opportunity is still there, and until they say "no," it's not over.

Objections can also clarify whether we've made a mistake and approached the wrong buyer. They give us the opportunity to point that person in the right direction and get on to the next buyer.

There are basically two kinds of objections: the ones you can see and the ones you can't, which I cleverly call *hidden* objections.

The objections you can see are usually some variation of three issues: *price*, *quality*, and *service*. These are fairly straightforward and lend themselves well to the strategies that follow.

Trickier, however, are the hidden objections, for obvious reasons. Unfortunately, these come up a lot and can make life painful. Hidden objections aren't necessarily logical. They're much more difficult to wheedle out and overcome, and they require lots of patience, often because the buyer isn't aware of them.

The temptation, of course, is to say forget it. If they're not going to approach this logically, I'm not going to bother with them. Yet everyone harbors hidden objections, and many times they can be the deal breakers.

Sometimes the hidden objections are incredibly illogical. The buyers don't like the way you look ("She reminds me of my ex-wife"); or they find your accent annoying ("He sounds like Colonel Klink"); or their own egos get in the way ("I shouldn't need a professional organizer to get my office into shape!").

Self-doubt is a common hidden objection; some people are just very indecisive. Sometimes the problem is simply that your competitor got there first, and the buyer is reluctant to tell you that.

The most difficult hidden objection to overcome is not really an objection at all: Sometimes buyers just don't know what they want. You may, in truth, be a godsend with exactly what they need to solve all their problems and live happily ever after, but they wouldn't know it if you wrote it in the sky with fireworks.

Which brings me to an important point about hidden objections: They're not your fault, and sometimes there's nothing you can do about them. You can listen carefully, watch body language, look for hidden clues, test theories ("Sometimes people find my accent somewhat difficult to understand, but I'm taking a speech course to deal with it right now"), and still never know what went wrong. You can't control what you can't control.

Overcoming Objections

When potential buyers express an objection, effective salespeople usually take one of the following approaches: They seek to overcome the objection with information, reassurances, warranties, and guarantees; or they try to outweigh the objection with benefits. Both strategies are based on looking at things from the buyer's point of view.

Using the former approach in, say, a job interview situation might go like this: "Yes, I'm looking for $10,000 more than you're offering, but we could structure it so that I receive the salary increments based on my production."

Using the benefits approach, the same situation might go like this: "The fact is, I do expect $10,000 a year more if you hire me for this job because I have an existing book of customers that I'm bringing with me."

When the objection is *price*, experienced salespeople point to benefits. Price objections are most often overcome by quality. It's not how much you're paying; it's what you're getting for your money.

Are You a Clerk or a Sales Professional?

I was standing at the jewelry counter recently, horrified by the price of some earrings I thought I wanted to buy. "My goodness, these are expensive!" I said to the gal behind the counter. "Yeah," she said, "they really mark this stuff up. I think these were on sale last week. Too bad you missed it."

Eeeeeyikes! Talk about failing to overcome an objection! Getting in agreement with me was no better

When the issue is quality, again most salespeople will point to benefits or will provide reassurances, such as warranties, to show that the product is a good one. A testimonial from other satisfied buyers never hurts.

Service concerns can also be addressed with guarantees and warranties. The idea is to show that you'll be there to back up the product.

Overcoming hidden or illogical objections is tougher. All you can do is listen carefully and try to hear what's *not* being said. Maybe the buyer has erroneous information, which you can correct. Maybe the buyer has too little information to make an informed choice. It takes patience and imagination to dig out this stuff, but it's worth the effort in the end.

Overcoming objections is never about strong-arming people. It's about listening to their needs and even putting them ahead of yours. You have to make their needs enough of a pri-

than telling me to take 'em or leave 'em. It was clear I wanted those earrings, but this *clerk* didn't have a clue how to tell me what value I would be getting for my money.

The ability to recognize and overcome objections is the difference between a salesperson and a clerk. Which one are you?

(P.S.: I ended up leaving the store and buying the same earrings somewhere else for nearly the same price.)

ority that you *notice* their concerns, take them seriously, and try to satisfy them.

Closing the Sale

This is the part of the sales process that separates the women from the girls—and it's where many of us cave in like a rain-soaked furniture carton. We work so hard to put together high-quality presentations, present ourselves as competent profes-sionals, listen like crazy to all the objections, and fend off every one, but then *never ask for the business!*

Appointment after appointment, interview after interview, and nothing.

Author Joe Gandolfo offers a terse but useful admonition on this subject in *How to Make Big Money Selling*:

Let's get one thing straight, you don't make sales presentations for the sake of entertaining people or informing them.
The only value of an aborted sales presentation is the experience you got out of it if you're smart enough to learn from
your mistakes. Your job is to help the prospect. The best way
to accomplish this is by helping them to buy your product.

Closing the sale has to do with being ready to get this
thing over with, from both the customer's point of view and
yours. What you're looking for is a signal. It can come at any
point during the process, so you have to be listening. It might
sound like "When might you be available?" or "Here's my budget for this product" or "How much could you deliver for this
price?" These are *closing signals*. When you hear them, it's time
to shut up and let the customer *buy*.

The real trick here is to get out of your own way. If you're
listening, you'll know when to stop.

Closing Techniques

Three tried-and-true closing techniques are the either/or close,
the urgency close, and the service close.

The Either/Or Close

When you use this close, you pick a likely spot during the presentation (preferably after you've received a clear closing signal), and you simply assume the prospect is going to buy and
that the only thing left to work out is when and how much. It
looks like this in a typical sales situation: "So, do you think you'll
be taking the blue one or the gray?" Or in a job interview situation: "Would you like me to start on the first of the month or

the fifteenth?" When you're planning your family vacation: "Would you like to go to Las Vegas or Bermuda this year?"

The Urgency Close

Use this to crank up the pressure a little bit. It looks like this in a typical sales situation: "This is our most popular item, and we often run out during the summer months. In order to serve you better, if you place your order now, I can assure its availability." (This is especially effective if it's true. Media salespeople, for example, do usually sell out during the last quarter of the year because of Christmas. So it's true scarcity.) In a job interview situation, it looks like this: "I am looking at offers from two other companies. When do you think you might make your decision?" When you're planning your family vacation: "These Club Med packages might not be available next year."

The Service Close

This focuses on making the process of buying as effortless for the prospect as possible. In a typical selling situation it looks like this: "Would you like that gift-wrapped?" or "Can I hold this for you?" or "May I ship this for you?" In a job interview situation, it looks like this: "I could use my bilingual skills to interpret the company brochure." When you're planning your vacation: "Here's a brand-new case for your passport, dear."

A final word on all of this: From the buyer's point of view, the selling process is about *risk*. I'm betting that whatever amount of money I'm spending, this is what you, the seller, says it is, and it's going to do what you say it's going to do. Selling, from your point of view as the seller, should be about decreasing the risk to the buyer. If you can do that, the rest will be easy.

If they can't understand it, they can't buy it.

BRIGID MCGRATH MASSIE

Developing a Winning Sales Approach
Selling As Communication

L et's begin this chapter with a statistic (no groaning!): 80 percent of our waking hours are spent in some form of communication. Think about that number for a minute. If, in an average day, we spend about eight hours sleeping (for moms, cut that to six; for working moms, shave off another forty-five minutes to an hour), that leaves us with sixteen hours during which we're up and about. Scoop out the time we spend commuting, sitting slack-jawed in front of the tube, or hiding out in the john, and that leaves us with around twelve hours. And *that* means we've got nearly ten hours waiting for us every time we crawl out of bed in which we will be *communicating*.

Good communication skills are a salesperson's greatest asset. Most of the sales seminars I teach are really communication skills workshops—and most of the time, the attendees are practically salivating for the stuff. I think the reason is that salespeople know instinctively how important these skills are. In a way, it's just common sense. If you don't connect with someone—if you don't *communicate*—you won't make the sale.

Yet most of what passes for communication in this culture is just the automatic, ritualistic exchange of words:

"Hi, Bob."

"Hello, Sally."

"How's it going?"

"Fine. How are you?"

"Fine."

"Well, you take care."

"You too."

Bob and Sally weren't communicating; they were just taking turns talking.

Here are two more stats (and then I promise I'll stop): The average manager spends 50 percent of her time on the job communicating; for the average salesperson, that percentage jumps to 75. So it's clear that successful salespeople must also be effective communicators. It is the essence of selling.

But what about everybody else? What about all those people who don't have "sales" in their job title? (Though, by this point in the book, we can hope they know they really are salespeople, too.) Without a doubt, your ability to communicate effectively affects nearly every aspect of your life. In many cases, it's a make-or-break skill. In today's workplace, it's just not enough any more to be technically competent or to have a lot of enthusiasm—though those things are important. All of us must be able to deliver and receive messages accurately. The ability to make ourselves understood and to understand others is absolutely critical.

If you really want to get that job, land that promotion, or influence that person or situation, you've got to hone your communication skills.

Do You Hear What I Hear?

Before you can deliver a message, you must be able to receive one. In other words, you have to *listen.* Bad listening lies at the root of most miscommunication, and it's an epidemic. Most of us simply talk too much, so the quick fix here is to just practice *shutting up.* But in some cases, bad listening comes from a long-held mind-set about the act of selling itself. It shows up in the used car dealer's callous close; the telemarketer's wooden, scripted words; and the retail salesperson's lackluster locution.

By far the most glaring example of bad listening in the sales world is the canned spiel. I shudder to think of it. (Really! If I were writing this by hand, some of the lines would be all squiggly.) There is no one size that fits all when it comes to human interaction.

Maria, a radio salesperson with a fairly good-sized market, is a classic example of bad listening because of a canned spiel. She called on Jerry, a store owner who had expressed some interest in buying some ads. Right away, Maria went into her spiel, as she always did, telling Jerry all about the station and the various programs it aired. Unfortunately for Maria, Jerry had been listening to the station for twenty-five years. He played it over the store's PA system all day long. He thought of himself as a loyal fan, and Maria's canned approach offended him. Not only did she not get the sale, but also, for awhile at least, Jerry turned the dial to another station.

If what you do is regurgitate the same speech all over again with every customer in every situation, you're as far from communication as the moon is from Miami. If you want to be an effective communicator, can the canned spiel!

Much as I'd like to, I can't say that the canned spiel never works. It does produce sales in some situations. But all too often, these sales result in buyer's remorse, returns, and complaints. Who needs those?

All of this really just amounts to common sense, yet so many people I talk with still cling to the idea that they have to cough up some predigested sales drool to do the job. "Look, Brigid," I'm often told, "I have to give my clients a certain amount of information in order for them to understand what they're doing."

Excuse me? How do you know that? How could you possibly know what that other person—probably a total stranger—knows or doesn't know, *especially* if what you are doing is talking instead of listening? The number-one sales question always has to be, "What do you have, and what do you want?" I can only sell them what's in the middle.

Careful listening yields a host of benefits that far outweigh the perceived benefits of the jabber-them-into-submission approach. It heightens awareness of alternatives and lessens assumptions. It keeps us light on our feet, ready for the unexpected, and focused on the other's satisfaction.

If we take this idea a step further—and I believe we must—careful listening to *ourselves* can yield tremendous benefits as well. What we hear and see is always colored by our own experiences and often does not reflect what's there at all. Listening to ourselves is an absolutely terrific way to ferret out these kinds of biases and filters—what amount to blocks to communication.

For example: You walk into a family-owned grocery store, and you hear your mind say, "Hey, this is a funky mom-and-pop operation. These people can't have much money." But then you listen to the customers, and you learn that this mom-and-pop operation has made these folks millionaires. You watch a shabbily dressed minority mom and her dirty kids walk into your shop, and you hear your mind say, "She's definitely a blue-collar type. No dough, no how." Then you listen to her and discover that she is a solidly upper middle-class woman who's been working in the garden with her children. You go to help a little old lady, and you hear your mind say, "She's going to want the cheap and dowdy stuff. And she's probably on social security. No point in showing her the higher price point items." Then you listen to her, and she asks for Guess?-brand jeans.

Good listening is the first step toward better communication. Without it, you're just talking to yourself.

Seven Communication Truths

The truth about good communication is that it's not easy. It takes some effort and imagination to develop skills in this area. You're probably going to have to change some habits, get yourself off autopilot, and fly this thing *awake*. The good news is that it's worth the effort. Every minute you spend developing your communication skills will pay you back many times in many ways in every aspect of your interactions with others.

So what exactly is it that I'm nagging you to develop? The following seven truths about communication should serve to further define the concept as I see it:

1. *If you don't think ahead about what you're going to say, you probably won't get your message across.*

We've all experienced how easily messages can be misperceived, even those delivered with the best of intentions. That's why it's so important to think ahead about what you are trying to communicate. Even something as innocent and well meant as a compliment can turn sour if you aren't clear in your mind about what you're saying and doing.

For example: Margaret is a manager in a small manufacturing plant. She is a hard worker, and for weeks she had been harried with the details of a new operations setup. She nearly let some important paperwork slip through the cracks, but thanks to her secretary, Jane, everything went out on time. Margaret was understandably grateful and stopped by Jane's desk to compliment her on her work.

"Hey, Jane," she said. "You're really doing a great job."

Jane forced a smile, nodded, and watched her boss furtively for the rest of the day, as though she were waiting for the other shoe to drop.

Before you decide that Jane was responding irrationally, you should know that Margaret's pattern was to ignore her secretary most of the time—until she needed a favor. Her amorphous pats on the back were often followed by avalanches of work for poor old Jane.

If Margaret had thought over her communication ahead of time, she might have made it very specific: "Jane, I want to thank you for getting the Broderick file out the door on time.

You saved me from having to stay here all night and miss my son's play. I really appreciate it."

Jane still might have cringed, as she was conditioned to do, but a more specific compliment might have focused Margaret's message enough that Jane would have really heard it.

The issues here are sensitivity and empathy for the person receiving your message. I'm not talking about creating a script but rather about investing in what often amounts to nothing more than a little forethought.

Ben, for example, is a Yellow Pages ad rep who likes to wing it when he makes presentations. This would be a good thing if he were also a good listener, but he's not. When he stopped to call on Dana at her flower shop one afternoon, it didn't bother him that he hadn't given much thought to what he was going to say. Unfortunately, he hadn't given much thought to the customer, either.

"This kind of ad is very important to your competitiveness," he said to her. "I just sold one to The Flower Boutique down the street."

What Ben failed to consider was how Dana might feel about her closest competitor. Had he thought about it, he might have been a little more wary. He might have asked her whether she had considered this form of advertising and whether she wanted to know what others in her industry were doing. And he might have made the sale. You see, Dana thought the owner of The Flower Boutique was an idiot, and she usually did the opposite of whatever he did.

Am I saying we should all walk around on tiptoes, never speaking an unconsidered word? Of course not. What I am saying is that the path between what we want to say and what actually gets heard can be a treacherous one, and we're bound to trip once in a while. Sometimes this results in nothing more than a skinned knee; other times we'll be lucky to not break our necks. Giving this process some up-front attention will save a lot on Band-Aids.

2. *Rehearsing your response weakens your message.*

Though communication is strengthened when we think ahead about what we're going to say, it is weakened when we rehearse our responses. I know this may sound like I'm giving two conflicting pieces of advice, but each is a different aspect of a single idea: *being awake*. In the first case, you are simply looking before you leap; in the second, you are eliminating preconceived notions—those biases and filters mentioned previously in this chapter—that create blocks to communication.

When you rehearse your responses, you stop listening. When you stop listening, you stop communicating. You're also much more likely to answer questions that haven't been asked. You might end up reading the script for an entirely different movie.

Going into a sales situation script-free also give you an opportunity to improve your listening skills. If you're clear about what you're doing, if you know your product/service/point of view, and if you just pay attention to the other person, you'll know what to say in the moment.

3. *It takes at least two media to get your message across.*

People learn and retain information in a variety of ways. Some of us are visual learners; some are auditory. Some of us are experiential. Some of us respond well to the written word; others prefer pictures, charts, and graphs. So, in any selling situation, your odds of communicating your message are a lot better when you have at least two ways to communicate your message.

Does that mean you have to come in with a dog-and-pony show? Not unless you're in the pet and livestock business. What it does mean is that since you don't know how the other person best retains information—she may not know herself—you'll want to cover at least two bases. Business cards, product samples, brochures, newspaper and magazine clippings, an audiotape or videotape: All of these things are going to increase the chances that your message gets through. In nonsales situations (are there such things?), such as a job interview, you might leave behind your resume.

Jake, an architect I know, goes at this in a unique way. He takes gorgeous photographs of the completed buildings he designed, then sends them out to all of his former clients with a caption like "Proud to be a part of the Such and Such High School project that will serve the class of 2000." He makes a special effort (not that much work, really) to include his clients in his work and his life and to give them good feelings about having hired him. The recipient's of Jake's photos feel a lot of pride at being included in the mailing, and they're glad to be in the know about what's going on around town. Do you think Jake ever has problems with referrals?

Remember how easily verbal communications run astray. One of the situations in which I've seen this happen with shocking frequency is in performance appraisals. People will tell me, "Brig, I walked in there, and the guy bludgeoned me to death!" Then, when I ask them what their rating was, sometimes I hear that they were rated outstanding. What happens in these cases is that the appraisee is under a lot of stress, making it much more likely that he or she will misinterpret the appraiser's message. The verbal communication by itself is much weaker. (In fact, many employers are afraid to put very much down in writing during performance appraisals that they can be held to later. Personnel records do get subpoenaed all the time, so employers are right to be careful, I suppose, but it sure leaves a lot of people guessing about what the heck is going on.)

In many situations, the only collateral you've got is a business card. But don't underestimate its importance; business cards are essential and can be very useful indeed. They provide one more way to connect with someone and open up the lines of communication. (Here's my patented business card test. Every business card must be free of any handwriting, be readily accessible—women with cluttered purses take note—and be given out without apology or explanation of any kind. Nobody cares if the company has changed its colors or logo or that *this* isn't your current title.)

The sales rep of a major hotel chain once asked me exactly when the best time is to hand out a business card. For me it's as soon as possible. We all know what a challenge it is to remember the names of people we've just met. Handing out the card early in the meeting gives the other person something to refer to so they won't forget you, and they can relax.

4. *If they can't understand it, they can't buy it.*

"Well, Ms. Massie," the guy at the computer warehouse said, "you don't have enough RAM to operate your CD-ROM, and you'll need a SCSI and a newer version of DOS, and we can see that there are some problems with the HIMEM.SYS, AUTOEXEC.BAT, and CONFIG.SYS files. Oh, and while you're at it, you might as well pick up a super VGA."

Okay . . .

Later, at the bank, a vice president smiled at me and said, "Once you buy your IRA and then use your PAC money, you can beat the IRS rules on the COBRA requirements."

Uh-huh . . . I smiled back and said, "Well, okay, but let's do it on the QT, PDQ, or we'll be SOL." Then I hurried away in search of people who use words with a reasonable number of vowels in them.

Every business and every industry has its own language, its own *jargon*. But it's insider stuff, not very inclusive, and frequently off-putting to potential customers who might not have an industry glossary with them. When it comes to jargon, I say bag it. Speak to people in English or in whatever actual human language is appropriate, but avoid like the plague your particular industry-ese.

When I say this in my seminars, I often hear from people who remind me that certain customers—for example, people who are professional or amateur sailors and buy from the marine products companies—like using industry jargon. They even judge the salesperson, they tell me, on how well he or she can use it. Okay, fair enough, but even then you have to keep in mind that your purpose is to communicate. Are they using those same terms back to you? Or do they begin to break off the conversation? Watch their body language. Are they blinking their eyes? Turning their heads? Shifting from one foot to the other or bouncing a crossed leg?

Some time ago I met with a television ad sales rep. I wanted to talk with her about buying some advertising for a group of businesses with which I was working. When we finished with the meeting, she said, "I'll get in touch with you and let you know the *avails*." Avails? She faxed me back a list of the times on various shows that were available. Oh. Avails. I get it. Of course, for her, it was to no avail—and no sale.

5. *Communication is a set of learned skills.*

If you're not communicating well, don't blame the gene pool. Communication skills are learned, not inherited. In my first book, *What Do They Say When You Leave the Room: How to Increase Your Personal Effectiveness for Success at Work, at Home, and in Your Life,* I wrote about the crucial communication skills we learn in school: reading, writing, and talking. (Talking? Oh, yeah. Don't you remember speech? Debate?) Most of the teacher's time is spent teaching people how to write, even though in the real world, most of us write very little; research tells us about 9 percent of our postgraduate time is spent writing. You spent between six and eight years learning about reading, and yet, after school is out, you'll spend only about 16 percent of your time in that activity. The time spent learning to speak and give presentations amounts to a couple of years at best. Yet professional people spend as much as 35 percent of their time at work talking—to coworkers, employees, supervisors, customers, venture capitalists. But worst of all, and in my opinion the reason we have a communication crisis in this country, no more than six months is given over to the development of *listening* skills, an activity in which we spend roughly 40 percent of our time.

6. *Less is more.*

If you're listening—the most important element in successful communication—you aren't talking much. But that's as it should be. Good communication is lean and focused. Remember, if someone is not comprehending you, elaborating is probably just going to make things worse. Flapping your lips may move some air, but it won't get you any closer to your goal.

In his wonderful book *How to Get Your Point Across in 30 Seconds or Less*, Milo O. Frank observes that the average person's attention span is about thirty seconds long. He also puts together some important basic principles of lean communication, which I paraphrase here:

- The message must convey one clear-cut objective.
- The message must be directed at the right person or persons.
- You must know, in advance, as much as possible about the people with whom you wish to communicate, and you must use the right approach.
- Find a hook, a statement or object, used specifically to get attention.
- Use imagery: Think in pictures and use descriptive words your listener will remember.
- Use clear and simple language your listener will understand.
- Use an appeal that speaks to the emotions and touches the heart of your listener.

You will find Mr. Frank's readable book listed in the bibliography, along with other resources we hope you will find helpful.

The basic principles of lean communications, which we just restated, are applicable whether you're sending e-mail, talking on the phone, or communicating in person.

7. *You can't not communicate.*

Remember, 70 percent of the message you communicate is nonverbal. You can sit there on your hands with a tube sock stuffed in your mouth, and you'll still be communicating. People who sit silently tapping their pens on their desks are communicating. People who can't seem to keep eye contact are

Separate Realities

Effective salespeople know that, even when we're playing the same notes, we're not always on the same sheet of music. My favorite innocuous example of this comes right out of *Reader's Digest*: A mother was thumbing though a storybook, trying to find a story to read to her little girl. The little girl suggested opening the "menu" to see what the story book had to offer. "No, dear," the mother said, correcting her, "it's not a menu. It's the table of contents." Later the mother related the story to her

communicating. People who show up late and unprepared and never really say much are communicating.

What I'm talking about here, of course, is body language. There are a number of books out there on the subject of body language, but it's really just a matter of common sense and close observation. It's very important to look at your own body language. Watch your posture, make sure you have a firm but not overpowering handshake (avoid the limp shake at all costs); and don't sit with your arms crossed across your chest while saying, "I'm really into meeting people."

The Right Approach

The seven communications truths are very useful as a kind of preflight checklist. Use them to get yourself mentally together

own mother, remarking how interesting it was that her daughter had used a computer reference. The grandmother said, "I think it's because you've been taking her out to too many restaurants."

We all think we're communicating, but even when we use the same words, it's possible to be completely misunderstood. Customers will use words that are relevant to them, and they'll have whatever meanings they have. It's not up to us to "correct" those meanings but to understand them.

before you go out on a sales call, pick up the phone, or go in for that job interview. It's a highly effective way to get yourself focused and in motion; it prepares you to respond rather than react.

But you can't stop there. You also have to choose the right approach for that individual. As I said before, one size does not fit all; each situation is unique. The needs and interests of the individual to whom you are selling always dictate what you say and do.

This is also about maintaining a focused mind and a clear objective. No muddy thinking allowed! In *How to Get Your Point Across in 30 Seconds or Less*, Milo Frank addresses this issue. He offers several examples of clear objectives and appropriate approaches. When you try this yourself, remember always to state your approach in a single sentence. This forces you to focus.

Here are a few examples of this one-sentence approach to focusing on your sales mission:

EMPLOYEE TO BOSS
Objective: To get a promotion
Approach: A company must develop leaders to survive.

DISSATISFIED CUSTOMER TO SELLER
Objective: To get money back or an exchange
Approach: I know good companies like yours stand behind their merchandise.

EMPLOYEE TO BOSS
Objective: To get a raise
Approach: I've proved the value of my work to the company.

BOSS TO EMPLOYEE
Objective: To keep employee without giving him a raise
Approach: Everything in its time.

CUSTOMER TO CREDIT COMPANY OR BANK
Objective: To not pay incorrect charge
Approach: I'll be glad to pay when the charges are proven correct.

SALESPERSON TO CUSTOMER
Objective: To sell diamond earrings to customer for wife's anniversary
Approach: What better way to show you love her?

ONE BUSINESSWOMAN TO ANOTHER
Objective: To get her to talk to a franchise dealer

Approach: Financial independence for women is wonderful, new, and exciting.

CUSTOMER TO SALESMAN
Objective: To get the best buy
Approach: I like your product, but I'm on a tight budget.

NONSMOKER TO CIGAR SMOKER AT THE NEXT TABLE
Objective: To get him to stop smoking
Approach: I'm allergic to cigar smoke; it makes me ill.

Let's pause here at the end of this chapter for a short digression. (I'll try not to rant.) When I talk about finding the right approach to fit the situation, I inevitably hear from a few folks who throw the M word at me: *manipulation*. Their concerns are reasonable, given the stereotype of the sales profession in our society. Let me make myself clear here: I am not the least bit interested in teaching anyone how to manipulate. We have enough manipulators in this world without me contributing to the creation of more of them. What I am interested in is helping people learn to listen, to become more sensitive to other people's needs, and to develop a genuine concern for the other person's satisfaction. That's where the true joy of this endeavor lies. (There, that wasn't so bad.)

5

If you want to kill any idea in the world, get a committee working on it.

CHARLES KETTERING

Managing Effective Meetings

Y ou might wonder why I've included a chapter on managing meetings in a book about everyday selling skills. After all, there are entire books on the subject already in print. Not to mention that most of the salespeople I know hate meetings and avoid them whenever possible. In fact, most *people* I know hate meetings. Chances are, most of the meetings in your life are time vampires, draining the lifeblood from what might have been highly productive days.

Yet meetings are an unavoidable fact of life, in both our professional and our personal lives. I'm not just talking about the sitting-around-the-conference-table-while-Bob-from-accounting-reads-from-the-annual-report type of meetings. I'm talking about the morning you spent with your supervisors talking about the problems at the new plant; the lunch with your husband where you planned your vacation; the get-together with your staff about the office Christmas party; the job interview; the parent-teacher conference; the local fund-raiser; and the sit-down with your kids to talk about their grades.

The meetings in your life may be assets or liabilities, but it's clear they're not optional. Since they can't be avoided, they should not be ignored. Learning to orchestrate, conduct, and participate in meetings effectively is one of the most important everyday selling skills. Developing this skill takes you off autopilot and leads you to effective, productive time.

Routine Meetings

Just a quick comment about routine meetings: *Most are doomed to failure.* Meetings are a fact of life, and you can't avoid them, but if you can, do your best to stay away from those regular, weekly get-togethers with standing agendas. There are no greater time wasters. Many people in supervisory positions think it's important to get the staff together every Monday morning, whether or not they actually have anything to talk about. Maybe the idea is to create a space in which things can come up that otherwise wouldn't. Maybe they just like to see everybody in the same room. Whatever the reasoning, studies show routine meetings are useless beasts. Let's all work together to get these critters on the endangered species list.

To Meet or Not to Meet

Just because meetings are inevitable does not mean you can't or shouldn't try to trim down the number of meetings you call or attend. Meetings can be useful, energizing, clarifying experiences, but there are still just too many of them. People often call a meeting as a reflex or out of routine. More often than not, they fail to think through the reasons they wanted the meeting in the first place.

For example: With salespeople, almost every client or potential client contact is a meeting. Salespeople should certainly spend time with their clients, but they should be clear about why they're doing it. They should ask themselves, "Am I walking in here with the intent of getting an order, or am I just making a routine contact because the home office wants me to?" Maybe it would have been more effective to cut an article out of the paper, send it to the client, and have the "meeting" over the phone, by fax, via e-mail, or even through snail mail.

Remember, *a bad meeting is worse than no meeting*. Once you've had an unsuccessful meeting—gotten people together, disappointed them, confused them, or worse yet, bored them— it's really tough to get them back. It sets the tone for the whole relationship.

Meeting Checklists

Most of what follows is just plain old common sense. It comes from my own meeting experiences as well as the experiences of many clients, friends, and mentors. I would be remiss if I didn't make special mention of George David Kieffer and his excellent book *The Strategy of Meetings.* I highly recommend Mr. Kieffer's book, along with some others you'll find in the bibliography.

I've tried to make this a complete list of things you will want to do or think about to make your meetings work. For big, important meetings, you'll probably want to take all of these points into consideration. For short, informal meetings, you might need to address only a few.

Before You Decide to Call or Attend a Meeting

- Picture the outcome of the meeting.
  Some of the biggest time-wasters any of us faces are unscheduled appointments or unplanned meetings with no outcome planned. So, once you've decided to have the meeting, nothing is more important than knowing what you want to accomplish. Similarly, job interviews in which the applicant's objective is not clearly to get the job inevitably go nowhere. This is your most important step.

- Force yourself to justify the meeting as the best use of your time and the time of others.

- Make sure you can be ready for the meeting.
  If you plan to have a staff meeting and what you want is for everyone to go out and sell more, be prepared to answer the questions "What is more?" and "What tools will they need to accomplish that?" It could be the difference between a successful meeting in which the participants walk out motivated and on track or one in which they leave confused and offended.

- Ensure you have the authority to do what is requested.

- Make sure you really need a *meeting* to accomplish all of what you want to accomplish.

- Consider saying "no" to scheduling, conducting, or participating in the meeting.

- Consider a shorter and less formal get-together as an alternative.

- Prioritize the proposed issues and handle only some of them.

- Be ready to participate fully.
  Remember, you called the meeting. You are responsible if you waste the attendees' time, and they will hold you accountable. Judgments will be made, and you risk your credibility if you handle it badly.

Before the Meeting

Once you've decided to call or attend a meeting, take the time beforehand to prepare. Here are some things you should do:

- Be sure you clearly understand the stated goal or purpose.

- Be sure everyone you invite understands the stated goal.

- Agree among yourselves how you will measure success or failure.

- Invite the minimum number of people necessary to accomplish the goal.

- Streamline the number of issues to only those necessary to accomplish the goal.

- Prepare in advance. Visualize the meeting as you would like it to take place.

What If They Had a Meeting but No One Came?
The greatest waste of time I can imagine is a meeting with the wrong people. Salespeople know what this is like, yet many continue to get sucked in time after time. Come in! Sit down! Glad you could make it! Everyone's here—except the decision maker, the one with all the relevant information, and the one with the money.

For example, Fernando, a merchant in a small shopping center with which I once consulted, decided the thing the center needed was television advertising. So he

- Create a hospitable, comfortable meeting environment. (Don't underestimate the power of donuts!)
- Establish a clearly worded agenda and get it out as soon as possible.
- Make tactful reminder calls or send faxes or e-mail.

During the Meeting
- Approach the meeting and all attendees with a positive attitude.
- Arrive early and greet everyone.
- Pay attention to where you sit. If you want to communicate more authority, sit at the head of the table. For building a team, sit somewhere in the middle.
- Reflect a positive attitude toward the task. Avoid sarcasm!

called a center-wide meeting, which all the other merchants attended. The only person he forgot to invite was a sales rep from a local TV station! So he set up another meeting and invited a local TV sales guy. At that meeting he and his neighbors learned that what everyone thought was a $500 idea was, in fact, a $5,000 idea. Later they decided to have a meeting about billboards.

Aaaaaarrrrrrrgh!

Thousands of hours and dollars are wasted on these kinds of meetings every year. Take a stand against them and refuse to attend!

- Make sure someone takes notes.

- If you're leading, start on time and begin forcefully.

- If you're leading, state the purpose and gain agreement on the time for completion. This is really crucial. Restate the purpose when the meeting starts to go off track.

- As leader, make sure everyone has a chance to contribute, clarify agreements and disagreements, and make people feel important!

- As a participant, contribute early, clearly, and often—but thoughtfully.

- Break up big problems into smaller, manageable pieces and address them separately or set them aside for research.

- Separate the issues discussed from the people presenting them.

Laid Back or Laid Out

Some of the companies where I conduct trainings explain to me in advance that their corporate culture is somewhat "laid back." Even now I cringe at the sound of that phrase! Whenever I hold meetings or seminars at these laid-back outfits, we fall pretty quickly into what I call the *restart mode*: Four people are there when I arrive, and we start the meeting. Then another person comes, and we stop what we're doing to bring him up to speed, effectively restarting

- Throughout the meeting, summarize what has occurred and its relevance to the goal.

- Make your own points clearly and concisely. Don't ramble!

- Avoid being argumentative. Know when to quit.

- Look for every opportunity to show courtesy and respect.

- Listen attentively and demonstrate your attention to others.

- Be there in mind as well as body—give 100 percent.

- Summarize what was accomplished in a positive way and thank people for their attendance.

- Don't allow the meeting to go on when its work has been completed.

After the Meeting

- Publish the proceedings as agreed.

the meeting. Later a few more wander in, and we restart again. And we do it again, and again, and again . . .

This is expensive, annoying, and disruptive behavior that no company should tolerate. And it's a huge problem. Companies are training their people to be late. They're showing them that there aren't any consequences for wasting other people's time. Folks, this is simply *not* how business is done. Nowadays I make it a policy to start on time and lock the door!

- Assess the meeting in terms of your original goal and your measurement of success. Keep moving toward the goal.

- Share the results with people who attended as well as with those who were unable to attend.

- Follow up on assignments quickly by indicating the responsible person, the task agreed to, and a deadline.

- Thank the participants again.

Creating an Agenda

Creating an effective agenda is truly an art. It's also critical to the success of formal meetings, such as meetings of boards, commissions, or clubs. But an agenda—think of it as a clear idea of what the meeting is about—is important in even the most informal encounters.

Whether you're sitting down to create a formal agenda or just structuring your thoughts on the fly, keep the following in mind:

■ *Less is more when it comes to agenda items.* When people sit down to compose an agenda, there's a tendency to include too many items. Be reasonable. What items will give us the greatest return for our investment of time and energy? Are some items better dealt with at another time? With different people?

■ *Avoid the "conquer world hunger" agenda.* I'm not sure there is such a thing as a meeting that's too short, but an agenda with incomplete information is almost worse than none at all. I'm not saying you should rack your brain to come up with 200 agenda *items*. I am suggesting that if you've decided an item is important enough to appear on your agenda, be certain you include enough information so the attendees can make meaningful contributions on the subject. And make sure the agenda items are limited enough to be doable within the framework of the meeting and by the participants you have so carefully identified.

■ *Make the agenda available in advance.* Most people just make up a laundry list of agenda items, then pass them out at the beginning of the meeting. But this doesn't give the meeting attendees time to prepare. The most common reason meetings fail is that participants don't have a clear understanding of the meeting's purpose. The second most common reason is that attendees haven't been informed in advance, so they're just not ready to contribute.

Your agenda should be circulated enough in advance to allow everybody to review it. Attendees may also want to do a little homework, so allow time for that, too. But don't distribute your agenda so far in advance that it will lose its urgency and get laid aside and forgotten.

■ *Identify the outcome expected of the agenda items.* This indicates to the participants whether the item is for information, discussion, action, or all three. Indicating the targeted outcome of each agenda item lets the participants know what is expected. People like to attend meetings that are dynamic, action oriented, and productive.

In *The Strategy of Meetings*, George Kieffer proposes the kind of crystal-clear agenda format that ensures a productive and positive meeting. Here's how that same agenda could be expanded:

1. Minutes: Approval of minutes of meeting of January 15, 1995. This is an ACTION ITEM. Minutes attached.

2. President's remarks: DISCUSSION ONLY. Report attached.

3. Budget for 1995: ACTION ITEM. Budget included. The 1995 budget was approved by the finance committee at the December meeting. Action by the full group was deferred at the December meeting, pending only receipt of a staff report regarding the Johnson program, which appears on page 10. The staff report, preceded by an executive summary, is enclosed for your review. Staff recommends approval.

4. Report on conferences: DISCUSSION ONLY. At its October meeting, we requested a report by staff, enumerating the various conferences to which we are invited to send a representative, as well as an analysis of the strengths and weaknesses of particular conferences. The report is

attached. It is the intention of the president to recommend action at the next meeting.

5. Committee reports

6. Finance committee: ACTION ITEM. The report of the committee is attached. Recommended action appears on page 1 of the report.

7. Long-range planning: A draft report is attached FOR DIS-CUSSION. The final report is expected to be approved by the committee at its meeting in two months.

8. New business

9. Adjournment

For getting things done in a group setting, there are few alternatives to a good meeting. With a structured but flexible agenda, the "right" participants, and careful staging, meetings can make all participants feel productive, included in the decision-making process, and "sold" on any actions on which participants are agreed.

6

A good speaker usually turns out to be someone who says exactly what you wanted her to say.

ANONYMOUS

Potent Presentations
Influencing People from One to One Thousand

I'm usually pretty good about admitting my own ignorance. I have an abundance of bad habits, it's true, but kidding myself that I know something when I really don't has never been one of them. So when my husband surprised me one day with a canister of pepper spray he wanted me to carry in my purse for self-defense, I held no illusions about my expertise in this area. What the heck was I going to do with this thing? I'd be lucky not to blast the clerk at the grocery store when I pulled out my checkbook!

That's why I found myself one Friday night a few weeks later sitting on a cold metal folding chair in a high school gymnasium with about two dozen other women, all proud new owners of their own self-defense condiments. We were there to get the hot skinny on the then-new pepper sprays from a police officer who traveled around the country giving talks on the subject. While the officer was knowledgeable, communication was not his strong suit. Less than halfway through his presentation, I considered giving myself a little pepper spritz just to stay awake. And I was not alone.

Officer Pepperman began his presentation by talking about the Saracens of ancient Greece and how they used to smoke out their enemies with . . . well . . . smoke. From there he took us on a truly mind-numbing stroll through the history of warfare that had absolutely no relevance to the group before him. Most of us were busy working women who just wanted a few tips on the best way to nuke a mugger with our little sprayers and then go home. Unfortunately, the officer never stopped to ask us why we were there, preferring instead to drag us through his carefully prepared but irrelevant lecture. He failed to realize that an effective presentation, like all communication, is a two-way street.

A Speech by Any Other Name

The ability to give effective presentations is an often-neglected but vital skill that can be crucial to your selling success. Whether you're talking with one person or speaking to a thousand, the level of your influence is directly proportional to your ability to get people to listen to you.

Right about now you're probably saying, "Wait a minute. I know what's she's talking about. It's . . . *gulp* . . . public speaking!" Okay, you're right . . . sort of. I have, in fact, inserted the word *presentation* where you might usually find "speech," but I'm not just trying to slip something past you with euphemistic language. Since selling is about communication, and most of the speeches I—and you, too, no doubt—have had the misfortune to sit through have had little to do with that concept, I want to distinguish between a speech as it's typically given and what we're dealing with in this chapter. Most speeches are little more than condescending pronouncements pushed at us from a distant lectern.

We tend to neglect our presentation skills, because most of us would rather have dental surgery sans anesthetic than speak in public; some of us would rather die. Public speaking consistently ranks just above death on those lists of things people fear most. But I'm convinced you cannot effectively influence others in everyday selling situations if you neglect this stuff.

No one expects you to become Earl Nightingale or Tony Robbins, but whether you're in a one-on-one situation or standing before a seething throng, you will deliver better presentations and enjoy them more (or at least hate them less) if you make an effort to acquire the skills and habits of a good public speaker.

A Radical Notion

In this chapter we will look at a few basic principles that, with a little practice, will greatly improve your presentations and your overall sales effectiveness. But before we get to the nuts and bolts, I'd like to talk about a slightly radical notion I have about this process.

As I've said, most presentations are delivered through what amount to one-way pipelines with little or no concern for those on the receiving end. But what is true of effective selling is also true of effective presentations: Both are about communication, and communication is always a *two*-way street. Therefore, *good speakers are also good listeners*.

Wait a minute! How can a *speaker* be a *listener?* Isn't she the one who's doing all the talking?

Yeah, but if she's really doing her job, she also asks a lot of questions before, during, and after the presentation, and she watches her listeners like a hawk with binoculars. She is *other focused*. In my experience, most of the fear associated with public speaking grows out of a self-focus that is utterly incompatible with this process. (More on this later.)

Before I stand up in front of a bunch of strangers and regale them with my stunning insights, I always ask the sponsors of the event a lot of questions: How long will the conference last? What other topics will be covered? What did you do last year? What kinds of people will be attending? I find out everything I can about the environment in which I'll be speaking and the people to whom I'll be speaking. Then I ask myself, "What would I want to hear on this topic if I were one of the folks sitting out there?"

Once I begin my presentation, I pay close attention to the audience. I never let my need to cover my material distract me from the people *with whom I'm trying to communicate*. I stay *other* focused. I watch their reactions, their body language. I take the measure of their energy level. And I ask them questions. Many's the time I've been up there, ready to forge ahead into the next section of my presentation, when I've been struck by the thought, "Are these guys really listening to me? Is this really what they want to hear right now?" Whenever that thought hits me, I stop, take a breath, and *ask* them about it.

For example: I was about ten minutes into a presentation called "16 Ways to Manage Your Stress" when I began to get the feeling the audience had stopped listening. I saw glazed eyes, slumped postures, and doodling. I caught a yawn or two out of the corner of my eye. So I stopped where I was and asked them, "What sorts of stresses are you dealing with in your lives right now?"

The simple act of asking a question instantly began to transform my presentation. I could see right away that the stresses they were really concerned about were numbers 11, 12, and 13 on my list. Rather than force them to sit through a bunch of talk they weren't going to listen to anyway, I shuffled a few papers and got right to the good stuff—the stuff to which they could immediately relate. Along the way, a woman stood up and told us about a seventeenth way to manage stress. That seemed to interest everybody, so I worked it into the presentation that day. The room became energized.

By shifting gears and responding to the reality of what I saw and heard, I was able to elevate my presentation from a *lecture* to a *communication*. By being a good listener, I became a better speaker. I was able to give my audience something they really wanted, and we all had a great time. Had I done what Officer Pepperman had done and simply plodded along with my prepared talk, it would have been an entirely different experience for everyone.

We've talked about the importance of effective listening and the dangers of relying on canned sales spiels in one-on-one presentations. Why should those issues be ignored when we make presentations to groups of people? Clearly, they shouldn't.

If what you're after is effective communication, your job is to figure out what your audience already knows and what it is they want to know. And the only way you can do this is by listening.

The 99 Percent Solution

The Boy Scouts say it best: "Be prepared!" Preparation is 99 percent of the battle when it comes to giving effective presentations. Failing to take the time to plan ahead, to consider potential problems, and to really get yourself ready for a presentation is the quickest way I know to crash and burn. To keep my presentations airborne and on course, I've devised the following preflight checklist:

I. THE PLACE
  A. Room size
  B. Seating layout
  C. Speaker placement
  D. Lighting
  E. Temperature
  F. Equipment
    1. Outlets
    2. Tables
    3. Screens
  G. Sound
    1. Microphones
    2. Sound system
    3. Acoustics

II. **THE PEOPLE**
  A. Number
  B. Education level
  C. Reason for being there

III. **THE PRESENTATION**
  A. Become an expert
  B. Keep it short
  C. Personal introduction
  D. The basics
    1. Introduction
    2. Highlight main points
    3. Cover main points
    4. Send a closing signal and summary

IV. **THE PERSON**
  A. Voice
  B. Facial expressions
  C. Body movements

Now, let's look at each of these categories separately.

The Place

It's really mind-boggling how many external factors can sabotage an otherwise effective presentation. I can think of dozens of instances in which a speaker has researched his audience, honed his presentation and his personal communication skills, checked over his equipment and the room layout, and then shown up at the venue only to find the air conditioner fan is so loud no one can hear him. Or the lights are so dim no one can see his great visual aids. Or the curtains won't make the room dark enough to show the slides. Or there is no extension cord for the slide projector. Or no table to set it up on.

It's your responsibility to check out the venue and deal with any external problems that might mar your presentation. Professional speakers often send out checklists to facilities managers, but the real pros leave nothing to chance. It is, after all, their problem when the rap aerobics class next door starts shaking the light fixtures.

Show up at least an hour early; two is better. Look the room over. Ask yourself, "What are the roadblocks here between me and my audience?"

Start with the size of the room. Will the audience be crowded together or spread out? What can you do to compensate? Is there a better-sized room available if this one is too small or too large? It never hurts to ask.

How are the sight lines? Will everyone be able to see you easily? I've rearranged as many as 1,200 chairs that weren't set up properly! For one-on-one presentations, the optimal setup is side by side. When two of you are face to face, it can seem confrontational. Also, if you have a handout (and you'd better after reading Chapter 4), it's going to be upside-down for one of you.

In larger group situations, face to face is definitely the most comfortable. We've all been to those company dinners or Chamber of Commerce breakfasts where everyone is sitting at those wide, round tables. When the speaker steps up to the lectern, half the attendees have to turn their chairs and strain their necks to see her. That's what I call adult abuse! Conference tables are a little better, but the guys at the far end still have to crane their necks to see around the guys in front.

When it comes to seating arrangements, the idea is to make it as easy and comfortable as possible for your audience to see you. But sometimes you're stuck with a lousy setup. One way to compensate for bad seating is to move the speaker's location. Just because the lectern is fixed at the head table doesn't always mean you can't take your microphone and move to a better spot in the room. If there are posts or other sight line obstructions, you can move around a little, giving the cheap seats a chance to see you. Never *ever* stand behind a lectern that is taller than you are. No one can take seriously a disembodied voice.

How's the lighting? Will your audience be able to see your great charts and graphs? Will some people be blinded by glaring spotlights or the sun shining in east or west windows?

How about the temperature? This is very important. When people are too hot or too cold, they can't listen to you. Their discomfort negates even the most compelling content. I once gave a presentation in an abandoned bank building in which the heat hadn't been turned on. I had a dynamite presentation prepared, but people were getting frostbite! I could have been giving them the formula for eternal youth, and they wouldn't have heard a word I said, so I just cut things short and passed out the hot coffee.

It takes a while to adjust the temperature in a large room, especially one with a high ceiling, so deal with this issue right away.

Test the outlets, microphones, sound system, and any other equipment you will be using. Set up your slide projector and actually operate the thing. Slip a few of your transparencies into the overhead. And try out the sound system! Is it too loud, distorted, too quiet? Can you hear it in some parts of the room and not in others? Can you be heard without it? (In my opinion, this is better.) How long is your mike cord? Can you get to the slide projector or overhead with the mike in your hand?

Open Your Eyes and Ears Before You Open Your Mouth

Ed stepped up to the lectern and turned his smiling face toward us, the audience. He was a well-built man of fifty-plus years, with close-cropped, steel gray hair and a military bearing. He introduced himself as a professional motivational speaker, and he launched into his spiel. I'm going to motivate you, he told us. I'm going to give you my tips for being successful, tips that I culled from twenty-five years of military service.

Everyone around me suddenly looked depressed.

This was a professional business crowd, not a bunch of high school boys! No one in that audience could relate to the man or his message. Yet he was oblivious to

For many one-on-one appointments, much of this checklist won't be quite as relevant, but the principle remains useful. Ask yourself, "What are the impediments here to my giving an effective presentation?" For example: I always try to meet with people outside their offices, at coffee shops, or in conference rooms. If we stay in the office, I know I'm going to be interrupted by fifteen phone calls. It's hard for anyone to stay focused—listeners or speakers—with constant interruptions.

In other situations you have even less control over the environment. At a job interview, for example, you are essentially in the interviewer's hands. But you sometimes have a choice of chairs or other factors that can, if you're paying attention, make your presentation more successful.

the raised eyebrows and shifting rumps writhing before him.

Though our speaker was sincere, we were not motivated. We didn't want to be among the few, the proud, the whatever. The man even worked the room afterward, saying he hoped he'd given each and every one of us the shot in the arm we needed. He hadn't.

I'm not sure what Ed could have done had he taken the time to take the temperature of the crowd with a few preliminary questions. He and we were so mismatched I'm not sure the presentation could have been saved. But this example illustrates how important it is to know your audience in advance and to make your remarks relevant to them.

If you're going to give a presentation at an association meeting, say, the Rotary Club, attend a meeting ahead of time and watch how things go. What's it really like? Are people going to be eating while you're talking? If they promise you a half hour, are you really more likely to have only twenty minutes?

Not all external factors affecting your presentation are within your control. Even with the best pre-presentation reconnaissance, you sometimes just have to go with the flow. In other words, stuff happens. Here's my favorite example: I was scheduled to make a merchant education presentation at a shopping center a few years ago. The venue was the center's Chuck E. Cheese restaurant. (I'm sure most parents out there are familiar with Chuck E.'s. For everyone else, it's a theme pizzeria for kids, with games, activities, and mechanical bears a la Disney who come to life periodically and "play" songs.) The new owners, who had just taken over management of the place the night before, had gotten there early, brewed up plenty of coffee, and set out croissants. Everything looked great. Unfortunately, they hadn't yet familiarized themselves with the workings of Chuck E. and his pals. In particular, they *hadn't found the off switch*. No sooner did I start my presentation than Chuck E. and friends sprang to life with a rousing rendition of "Happy Birthday." The first time it was funny, and we all just laughed it off. But it soon became obvious that Chuck and the gang were going to be a permanent part of the festivities—every fourteen minutes! Bears singing! Antlers on the wall waving! Hooves clapping! Flags flapping! It was a nightmare.

I could have thrown up my hands and rescheduled, but it was really nobody's fault, and giving in would have been worse. What the situation called for was a sense of humor. Every time Chuck and the boys cranked it up, we just took a little break. That was when I coined the phrase "Does anyone have a short question?"

The People

The people who will be listening to your presentation are the most important part of it, so find out everything you can about them. Will this be a large group? Are they here voluntarily or at management's order? Is this a topic they've asked to hear about, or is this the boss's idea? Are they blue collar, pink collar, or white collar? Are they getting to play hooky from their jobs, or is your presentation putting them behind in their work? Are they on the clock, or is this on their own time? Assume nothing. *Ask*. The more you know about your listeners, the better your chances of connecting with them.

Start with their actual numbers. You have to know how many handouts and other collateral materials to bring. There's nothing more annoying than having to share a handout. It leaves people with the distinct impression you don't know what you're doing. This is especially important if you have highly detailed materials.

The rule of thumb about group size is the smaller the group, the higher the need for participation. Great throngs don't seem to have much need to interact with a presenter; an intimate gathering is no place for a theatrical presentation.

My advice is *be situational.* Adapt your presentation to the situation at hand. Otherwise, it's a dead giveaway that your presentation is canned.

The Presentation

There are a lot of books out there telling you how to write a speech. Since most speeches I hear aren't very effective and since we're talking about *communication*, I'd like to throw in my two cents on the subject.

The first and most important thing you can do to create an effective presentation is to become an expert on the subject. This is essential. Thorough knowledge of your subject frees you from your notes. Questions not covered in your outline won't throw you. You can relax, focus on your listeners, and do some listening of your own.

The second most important thing I want to say about presentations is to *keep them short.* Attention spans are truncated nowadays, even among people who are there because they want to be. In my fourteen years as a professional public speaker, I have never heard a single complaint about getting out early.

But it's not just that people's attention spans are short. Most of us simply don't want to know everything there is to know about a subject—not that you could tell everything anyway. Besides, adults don't generally come to a presentation knowing nothing at all. I'm no mechanic, but when I go to buy a new car, I'm not completely ignorant. I've talked with friends and family about it and read the latest issue of *Consumer Reports* on the subject. And it won't be the first time I've done it, either. Any car salesman who treats me like a moron will quickly lose my business.

Also, when you run long, it doesn't give people enough opportunity to go to the bathroom, to make their phone calls, or to get outside for a cigarette. And they don't get to move around and meet people, which is probably the reason most of them are there.

Just remember: Keeping it short does *not* mean talking faster! One of the most common mistakes I see among neophyte presenters is trying to cram too much information into the time allowed. Here's a rule I'd like you to take to heart: Practice your presentation with a stop watch, speaking at a normal rate of speed, then knock off about five minutes' worth of material. Never—*never*—speed up to get everything you've prepared into your half hour. If it looks like you're going to run over, dump something.

Third, always start off with an introduction. If you can't get someone else to do it for you, take a minute to tell the audience or client about yourself. I can't emphasize enough how important this is. You must establish your credentials before anyone is going to listen to the content of your message. While you're telling them all about job safety, the economy, or how to get the most out of the latest copy machines, they're wondering, "Who is this guy?" And that means they're not listening.

Even if you're a well-known figure in the company (say, the plant manager) or in your community (say, the mayor), never assume people know you. Even media stars who have performed for millions get an introduction. When Sally Struthers makes an appearance to talk about starving children, someone introduces her and tells the audience that she is the actress who played Gloria on *All in the Family*. Why? Because a heck of a lot of people never watched that show, and those who did might not recognize her outside the context of the show. Then the audience is told she has been working for many years to feed the hungry, traveling around the world to starving countries, and working with a number of charities. That answers their next question, and they can now pay attention to what she has to say.

In one-on-one presentations, the same rule applies. People want to know who you are and why you're qualified to be there. A short commercial will do: "I'm happy to discuss a radio advertising program with you. I've been with the station for ten years, so I know a lot about it." Never assume that people will automatically give you the credit you deserve until you've shown them your credentials. "I'm a brain surgeon with ten years' experience with this procedure, and I've saved the last ten people who came to me with your problem." Boom. Now you're more than some guy in a white coat, and your client can relax.

Think of it as flashing your badge. The cops know that "Freeze!" must always be accompanied by "Police!" if they expect to get any cooperation.

Beyond these three points, my advice is to stick to the basics of presentation structure, which are as follows:

Introduction
Tell clearly and simply what your presentation is all about. *Include a "hook," some intriguing bit of information that makes them want to hear more.* (Sounds a lot like a benefit, doesn't it?)

Highlights

Tell them what you're going to tell them, in a snapshot. Then tell them how you're going to go about it. Numbering is always useful here. It gives a shape to your presentation: "Eight Ways to Manage Your Stress" or "The Top Ten Marketing Mistakes." This helps everyone to follow along, so they know where they are in the presentation (you, too).

A quick warning here: Never go much over ten things. People are so bombarded with information these days, they're not going to remember much of what you tell them. Even when I have a higher number in my title, I usually break things down into about three main points. I once went to hear a speaker who gave a presentation called "110 Mall Marketing Strategies." To everyone's horror, she went through all of them!

Point-by-Point Presentation

The body of your presentation should cover the points you highlighted in your introduction. Don't beat it to death, but don't be so cryptic they have to guess what you're getting at or the implications of your message as they pertain to them.

Close

You've got to let them know that you're winding things down. Abrupt "that's it" endings can leave an audience or a client cold and confused. "That's about all we have time for today" gets them ready to go.

Always include a closing summary, especially if your topic was even a little bit complicated. It gives people a chance to get their minds around the things you've said and reconsider earlier points in the context of the whole presentation.

Then always take questions. Make it okay to ask by saying, "What questions do you have?" This is your chance to get in anything you may have forgotten, especially if you had to jettison because of time constraints. It's also an excellent opportunity to get some feedback. If everyone expresses confusion about something or has the same question, you can use that information to improve your presentation.

One final very important point about the content of effective presentations: As with all communication, you're trying to connect on an emotional level with someone who is your equal. You are tying to persuade and influence. You want to instill good feelings in your audience or clients so they'll take in the information you're offering. You rarely, if ever, want to come off as a teacher, preacher, or authority figure. Nothing shuts off communication faster than taking a one-up position.

For example: A young woman I know came to me one day for some help with a presentation she had been giving on the subject of sexual harassment. Her problem, she told me, was that her audiences were turned off by the subject, and she was experiencing difficulty getting people to listen to her. She wanted me to help her package the topic so it would be more palatable.

"How do you start your presentation?" I asked her.

"Well," she said in a sweet, small voice, "I start by pointing out that sexual harassment is a rampant disease rotting the heart of American society and that everyone in the room is probably guilty of it. Then I tell them what the law says and what the penalties are."

"Oh," I said. "And what sorts of reactions do you get?"

"For some reason," she said, "people are always very hostile and defensive. I guess the subject just brings that out in people."

Cluelessness incarnate! No wonder she was having a hard time getting people to listen to her. Who could sit there and listen to a presentation that started out like that? I don't particularly enjoy being accused of something until I exhibit that behavior, and I'm sure no one else does, either. The problem clearly wasn't with the subject, which should be handled sensitively in any event; it was with the presenter and how she held her audience.

Amazingly, some of the sales presentations I see aren't much better. Leave your judgments out of your presentations, and you'll find your audiences are much more responsive. Let go to take control.

Visual Aids

Just a word here about visual aids. As we've said in previous chapters, people learn in different ways. Some are auditory learners, some are tactile, and some are visual. Therefore, visual aids can be a very important part of your presentation package.

People like handouts, but they don't like to be buried in paper. And they don't like too much detail. There's no sense giving them a script of your presentation. So keep things in outline form. Less is more when it comes to handouts.

People also like charts and other graphics you might display on slides or overheads. These can really enhance your presentation, but they must be kept clean and simple if you want anyone to make head or tail of them.

Another thing is that your visual aids should be *professionally produced*. If you are not a graphic designer, don't design your own graphics. Amateur collateral materials and visuals will make you look unprofessional and will undermine your presentation. Is that line drawing of a doggie in the corner of your handout really facilitating your communication, or is it casting doubt in the minds of your audience and clients?

I believe strongly in using professional graphic designers. Don't be swayed by these computer programs that promise to make presentation graphics easy to design. The templates they employ are used by hundreds of others. You want your own identity and a presentation that is customized to you and your audience.

The Person

The "person" to whom I am referring, of course, is you. While the external factors that can affect your presentation are important and must be dealt with, nothing is as crucial as the *internal* factors.

Whenever you give a presentation, you are both the delivery system and the message itself. It has been estimated that more than 70 percent of the messages we communicate are nonverbal. Think about that for a moment. All the work you've put into preparing your presentation, scouting the venue, and researching your audience will amount to nothing if you ignore the things with which you communicate—your facial expressions, body movements, eye contact, and so on.

We discussed visual aids and how important they can be, but in fact, *you* are your best visual aid—or your worst, depending on how much attention you pay to the following aspects of your personal presentation.

Voice

1. Always use a conversational tone. Even in large groups, people tend to be put off by theatrical locution.

2. Vary the rate, pitch, and volume of your voice; no one likes to listen to a monotone.

3. Avoid a rapid-fire delivery. We love it in old Frank Capra movies, and you can sure get in more material, but lightning lips will just confuse and irritate your audience.

4. Watch out for slurring, excessive swallowing, tongue clucking, teeth sucking, or mumbling. The audience should notice nothing about your mouth other than the words coming out of it. Those words should be clear and easily understood. If you have a speech impediment or a distracting accent, consult a voice coach. (They really can help.)

Facial Expressions

1. Maintain good eye contact. Eye contact is the way we connect with each other. Make a point of looking around at the people in the group to whom you are speaking and catching an eye here and there. Try not to favor one side of the room. Avoid darting looks and never stare over their heads. Make sure that any eye contact communicates acceptance. If you're in a one-on-one situation, be sure your eye contact doesn't come off as a psychopathic staring contest.

2. Smile once in awhile.

3. Stifle any distracting personal mannerisms. If you've got some kind of a tic, if you're constantly licking your lips, or you spastically jerk your eyebrows scalpward with every other word, your audience will watch your facial gymnastics and miss your presentation.

Body Movements

1. Maintain good relaxed posture and keep your weight evenly distributed over both feet. Don't be a lectern gripper.

2. Make gestures that support your presentation. Plan them out and make them clear and strong. Keep your hands out of your pockets.

3. Avoid distracting body movements. Pacing, shifting from foot to foot, bouncing on the balls of your feet, and grabbing at your necktie will dilute your message and distract your audience.

Other common distracting behavior that can hurt your presentations include reading from your notes instead of speaking directly to your audience, hiding behind the lectern, using incomprehensible jargon, and saying "uh" or "you know" until the audience begins looking around for a rope.

Using Video to Hone Your Skills

Does all this sound like more than you can handle on your own? Have no fear, technology is here!

There is no greater tool available for improving your presentation style than the video camera. It's better than rehearsing in front of a mirror, and it sure beats those nervous critiques from your spouse.

Taping your presentations is a lot like standing up in front of an audience. And it gives you the opportunity to sit back afterward and react to yourself much as your audience will. You can see your quirks and mannerisms and zero in on your trouble areas—those annoying hand gestures, slouchy posture, and all that *blinking*. I didn't know I did that!

Especially as you begin your work in this area, I think it's very important to give yourself the gift of a video dry run.

The Fear Factor

Most people harbor tremendous fears about giving presentations, especially to large groups. In some cases their fears can be physically debilitating. But I believe that in most cases, a little anxiety is not only harmless but can actually enhance your presentations.

People often ask me if I'm ever nervous before I give a presentation. Sometimes I'm *extremely* nervous. But I *like* nervousness. I think it adds a shine to the eyes, power and enthusiasm to the voice, and energy to the material. I think a speaker's nervous energy is picked up by the audience and energizes the event.

Still, nervousness is not something one should leave unchecked, even while embracing it. The following are my three favorite techniques for dealing with pre-presentation jitters:

Deep Breathing

Inhale through your mouth until you've filled your lungs, then release the air slowly through your nose. If you start to get dizzy, you're overdoing this.

Muscle Tensing

Make your hands into fists, squeeze your eyes tightly closed, and tense all your muscles just as hard as you can for a few seconds. When you slowly relax, you will release a lot of the tension that supports anxiety. You'll be much more relaxed.

The Broccoli Check

This is a quick preflight check: Where are the lectern, your notes, your pointer? How are your hair, your tie, your skirt? Is there a big, green hunk of broccoli stuck in your teeth? Go though that mental checklist one last time before you roll out there. Since you've already prepared, it's more of a reassuring exercise than anything else.

It's very important to remember that in any group presentation, people in the audience are imagining themselves in your spot. The very fact that you have the guts to stand up there earns you a lot of respect and sympathy. If you say you are going to speak on a particular topic, but you don't deliver, that's when you can get killed—and rightly so. But for the most part, the audience is usually on your side.

I've dealt with a few hostile audiences in my time, but they were almost never actually hostile toward me. It was usually about the subject, or the company, or something else. And I've *never* been heckled. Ask yourself when the last time was that you were at a presentation at which the speaker was actually ridiculed by the crowd (when the subject wasn't politics).

Most of the time the people are there because they want to be there. If you can help them, they are almost always grateful.

Conclusion

I've watched a lot of professional people spend their entire lives dodging the stuff we've covered in this chapter. And I've seen it hurt their careers. Don't let yourself fall into that trap. This isn't rocket science.

There are many places you can go to practice these skills. Toastmasters is my number-one choice, but don't pass up opportunities such as the United Way, chairing your company's blood drive, or even being den leader for Pack 206.

With a little effort and practice, you can adapt these skills to your selling needs. You will gain confidence and poise that will serve you well. And if you give it a chance, you might even enjoy it.

*Every person you meet, stumble across, or blun-
der into . . . whose name, address, and phone
number you have the grace to ask for.*

RICHARD NELSON BOLLES, AUTHOR OF *WHAT
COLOR IS YOUR PARACHUTE*, ON HIS DEFINITION
OF A "CONTACT"

Developing Strategic Relationships

Whenever I begin talking about the importance of developing strategic relationships, whether it's during a presentation to a large group or while I'm working one on one, people start to squirm. I've learned over the years that, for a surprising number of folks, this is a pretty touchy subject. To some it sounds like I'm getting into a little of the old-fashioned customer manipulation, the tried-and-true salesperson-as-people-user strategy. To others it just sounds like fancy talk for brownnosing.

I included a chapter on this subject in my first book, and I still hear these concerns whenever I work with (so-called)

The Right Mentor

To paraphrase Mark Twain, mentors are like the weather; everybody talks about them, but nobody *does* anything. Yet we can all seek out and select our own mentors.

Lupe is a good example. A young, ambitious Hispanic woman, she had launched a job search campaign in an effort to secure a permanent secretarial job, yet after *seven years* she was still working as a temp. She went on interviews, worked in a number of companies on a temporary basis, but couldn't seem to make the right impression or the right connection.

She would still be a temp today if she had not met Rosa. More than twenty years her senior, Rosa had been where Lupe was. But she had managed to create a successful career for herself—a career that was still expanding.

nonsalespeople. Yet neither of these concerns could be further from the truth. What I *am* talking about here are *professional associations* that you develop and maintain for your and the other person's *mutual* benefit.

The fact is, some of us have achieved more than others. There are people out there who have already accomplished, right now, exactly what we hope to achieve someday ourselves: fame, fortune, education, artistic status. There are people out there with knowledge, resources, jobs, and experience that we don't have. And we *need* those people.

Building strategic relationships is second nature to effective salespeople. They routinely come into contact with people

Rosa was able to talk straight with Lupe, give her a few facts of life, open a few doors, and push the young woman through them. She coached her and advised her. She told her to take some classes (Rosa herself was enrolled in several), and she helped her polish her presentation. In the end she changed the entire course of the younger woman's life and career.

You want to find someone you can really see has walked in your shoes, someone whom you will believe, and someone *you can't buffalo* with your excuses.

Lots of people seek advice and then just blow it off. But we all need the support and guidance of someone who's been there, someone we trust, someone we can't fool with our excuses.

from all walks of life, and they naturally think of them as resources. Your bicycle needs an overhaul; they know the bike shop owner. You dropped one of your mother's antique silver napkin rings down the disposal; they know a silversmith who specializes in unique repair jobs. You're looking for a job in marketing; they know ten VPs looking for a guy just like you.

They also know who can help them to achieve their goals (if they don't know, they find out), both professionally and personally, and they seek out these people. They are also much more likely than many other groups to seek out *mentors*, people who have already been there and don't mind teaching the tricks of their trade. This is one of the most important lessons we can learn from the world of sales. If you're new at your particular game, you'd be wise to seek out someone who knows the ropes and make her your friend.

Personal Versus Professional Relationships

Strategic professional relationships are not the same as personal friendships. Though a genuine friend can also be an important strategic resource, it's important to be clear about the difference. In personal friendships, we usually share interests and values, a level of vulnerability, and mutual support. The rule of thumb here is to cultivate friendships with nourishing, positive people who give as well as they get (see "Nutritious Friends" in Chapter 8).

But the same ingredients, which combine so well to form the firm foundation of a solid personal friendship, eat away the structure of a professional relationship like starving termites. The same openness and vulnerability result in absolute death.

In other words, a strategic professional relationship must include a high level of *containment*—which would undermine a true friendship. If you want your relationships to be effective and satisfying, you must be able to recognize which types they are.

Types of Professional Relationships

I'll leave personal friendships to the psychology books and concentrate here on the kinds of professional associations effective salespeople spend so much of their time cultivating. There are basically two types of people with whom we have professional relationships: maintainers and propellers.

Maintainers

Maintainers are people who can make us or break us. They come in three varieties: *keystone* or *core* people, *experts*, and *tangential helpers.*

The core people include secretaries, administrative assistants, and waiters—the folks who do the job when we aren't around. How we treat them determines whether they are part of an effective support network or a constant source of aggravation.

Experts include our colleagues, professional contacts, and others we respect and value—the people off of whom we can bounce ideas.

Tangential helpers are the subcontractors who, while not necessarily doing our jobs, take on essential tasks that make our jobs possible.

Propellers

There are two types of propellers: *mentors* and *role models.* Mentors are the hands-on folks who guide us and help us with opportunities and access. Role models are our heroes, people we will likely never meet, such as Abraham Lincoln, Gloria Steinem, or Mark Twain.

Three Steps to Developing Strategic Relationships

Personal relationships grow out of basic psychological needs; professional relationships grow out of goals. I've noticed that a surprising number of people not only don't recognize this important difference but also have no idea how to cultivate and maintain the latter, even though strategic relationships are essential to achieving nearly all of our goals.

Third-Party Support Is a Vital Stepping Stone

The image of the "self-made" man/woman/person is almost a sacred icon in this country. From childhood we're inculcated with stories about the "self-made" millionaire, the powerful industrialist who "pulled himself up by his own bootstraps," the top executive who "made it on her own." Never mind that this bootstrap business defies the laws of physics; the truth is that no one succeeds totally on their own. We all have help. We get it from parents, teachers, coaches, older siblings, friends—people who show us the ropes and open doors.

The following steps offer a guide for developing and managing strategic relationships:

Do Your Homework

There are all kinds of people out there who are richer, wiser, and more powerful than you are. But only a few of those people are really important to you strategically.

Few would argue, for instance, that Donald Trump, Bill Gates, and Steven Spielberg are rich and powerful individuals. But how much could any of these men help, say, a young artist to develop a personal painting style? I suppose any one of them could sponsor her or buy some of her paintings. But how much useful career advice could they give? What tricks of the trade could they offer?

Of course, effective salespeople have always known that third-party support is a vital stepping stone to success. Other credible, knowledgeable people can play instrumental roles in helping us achieve our goals. More importantly, they can introduce us to options we didn't know were available. Hey, we don't know what we don't know. A highly successful saleswoman I know, a top producer at the top radio station in its market, put it this way: "I'm successful at what I do, but I don't know what else there is—especially when it comes to my career."

That's true of all of us.

Besides, what are the chances a struggling young artist is ever going to meet any of these guys in the first place? Not very likely. But that's okay. She doesn't really need them. What she does need is to develop a few strategic relationships right in her own backyard. To do that, however, she's got to do a little homework. (And so do you.)

First, ask yourself, Who are the people who are strategically important to me? Are they young or old? Men or women? Peers or mentors? Are they in my community? Or in a local trade association or service organization?

Ask yourself, How much time do I have available to devote to outside commitments? What type of activities would I actually like? Investigate groups and activities in your area that might present opportunities to meet people who are strategically important to you.

Also, look for something outside your field of expertise and your comfort zone. If you are an accountant, don't expect to get much mileage out of a membership in your regional accounting association; you already know accountants! But if you join, say, the local chapter of Toastmasters, you are bound to meet people from a very different quarter of the community.

Don't just go for the brand names, either. Just because dear old Dad was an Elk doesn't mean you will shine in that organization. Get involved in something in which you really want to be involved; it's the only way you'll be effective in that activity. The idea is to get out in the open, to look good, and to meet people.

Gain Third-Party Support

Third-party support is the endorsement or sponsorship of those people who can give you a boost into an organization, club, job, or whatever area in which you are interested. Here are six strategies for gaining this kind of endorsement:

1. *Ask for it.*

I'm surprised how many people balk at the idea of making a simple, direct request for support. It's honest, straightforward, and about as manipulative as voting.

But to make it work, you've got to be specific: "Brigid, I'm going to interview for this new PR job next week. You've seen me perform well as the publicity chairman for the United Way. Could you write a letter documenting my accomplishments?"

What could be more honest than that? It's even more effective to write up something yourself for them to sign. If you're not specific enough when you ask for help, you'll get something that says you're a great person who is easy to work with, when what you need is something that mentions the three great television spots you produced.

Remember: This is not a personal relationship in which we are best buddies and anything I write will be okay by you. You need a specific recommendation. The more specific you are, the better people like it. If you ask for a general endorsement, people feel you are asking them to take on your whole life.

2. *Let them off the hook.*

You can't have an effective strategic relationship unless you are willing to receive all kinds of information, both good and bad. When you try to gain third-party support, you are going to someone who knows something about you and *may* want to recommend you.

And maybe they don't. It's really in your best interest to make sure that person feels free to tell you the truth. "Bob, you are in a position to know the level of effort we put into this project. It's important to me to document that. It's important that someone like you make that kind of endorsement. What I'd like to do is draft a letter and have you sign it. But if there's anything in the letter that you want changed, or you don't feel you share the sentiment and don't want to sign it, you need to tell me."

Whew! I know it's scary, but when you approach third-party support this way, two things happen: You let your potential supporter off the hook, which makes them feel better and gives you greater credibility, and you can get some amazing feedback.

3. *Make it easy for them.*

That's what you do when you draft the letter of recommendation. Offer to get them the phone numbers or addresses they need. Do whatever you can to make it easy for them to give you their support.

4. *Express your appreciation.*

Sometimes—more often than you might imagine—people aren't aware of the roles in which we see them. It's important to let the person from whom you are seeking support know that you value their endorsement and why. "I'm asking for your endorsement, Alice, because you are the premier bank president in town." *Who? Me?*

5. *Report back.*

This is absolutely the most crucial next step. If you ask to use someone as a reference on your resume, for example, call back and let them know that you got the job. But whether you get the job or not, call back. This, more than anything else you do, is what helps to create the trust and involvement that makes the relationship work.

Remember: Many people in these kinds of influential positions tend to feel used by others much of the time. This step is what makes the difference between calling on somebody with whom you have a strategic relationship and using them.

6. *Send thanks.*

This differs from reporting back, which usually takes the form of a phone call. Sending something in writing, a personal note of thanks, to those who have supported you is tremendously effective. There's just nothing like saying "thanks" in writing. It's concrete documentation that validates the value of their efforts on your behalf. And again, the higher up the socioeconomic ladder you are, the less likely you are to get many thank-you notes. So, if you do get help from Bill Gates, he'll probably appreciate a note more than you know.

Participate in Social Engagements

Social gatherings are golden opportunities to network and to begin building strategic relationships. So don't pass them up!

Often when I speak at all-day conferences, I notice that, though most people will attend the prescribed program from 9:00 to noon, they disappear at lunch only to return when the program resumes at 1:30. What a huge mistake these people are making! Here they are, attending a conference to meet other people, and they evaporate at the first sign of a nonstructured environment.

Folks, you've got to work the room! You can't sit in the corner with your group of six and expect to get the kind of contact that generates strategic relationships. Reach out to other people. Establish yourself as a presence in the room. And do your best to make the event a good time for everyone.

I recently listened to another consultant speaking on this very topic. Something she said stuck with me: "The most important thing you can do at a social engagement," she said, "is to walk up to someone and *pretend* you're interested."

The reason that stuck in my mind is that *it's one of the most cynical recommendations I've ever heard.* It told me more about the consultant than anything else.

I believe very strongly that you must be *genuinely* interested in others. It's easy to do, really, but it's just not something you can fake.

Be a Resource for Others

People constantly ask me, "Brigid, besides yourself, who's a good speaker who could address our organization?" Every chance I get, I endorse those persons in whom I have confidence. I don't worry about competition or feel threatened in any way, because I know that creating opportunities for other people really pays off for me in the end.

Whenever you can provide introductions or leads for others, you become a resource. Far from costing you anything, it demonstrates your access to power. It shows people that you are someone who is connected and knowledgeable, and it cements relationships with those you recommend.

Also, the good things you say about someone else say good things about you. They say that you can recognize someone else's competence and that you're good enough yourself to not be threatened by other high-quality people. If you say that someone is honest, for example, you are also saying that honesty is something you value, and people will infer that you are honest, too.

Remember: You don't have stand in the spotlight to stand out. Turning the light on someone else can be truly illuminating.

Offer Assistance and Help on a Professional Level

This is a tough one, and you may flinch when you read it, but if done properly, offering comments and criticism of colleagues is an essential part of developing and maintaining strategic relationships. But be sure to follow these guidelines:

First, always frame your comments in professional terms, offering assistance and help. Next, be sure to direct your criticism at behavior, not individuals. For example: My family decided to change dentists a few years ago. When our old dentist called us to ask why, I could have said just about anything, but I decided to tell him the truth. Why were we going somewhere else? We always had to wait too long for service in his office. I told him that I had mentioned it on several occasions, and nothing changed, so I decided to take my family's business elsewhere.

I ran into him a few weeks later, and to my surprise, he thanked me. He said he took my comments to heart, reexamined the management of his practice, and made some changes. "Your feedback," he said, "was money in the bank."

Another example that's not quite so innocuous involved a coworker with a serious alcohol problem. It had begun to affect her work, and all of us who worked with her just didn't know what to do. I mean, if we said anything, she was surely going to deny it and hate us all forever. In the end, we had an intervention that led our friend to get help. We had decided that, risky as it might have seemed, we owed it to our friend to tell her the truth.

Whatever you may think, people don't always shoot the messenger. Helpful criticism given in the proper spirit and with a little tact can strengthen a relationship tremendously.

Seek Advice and Counsel

This isn't a pathetic, on-your-knees, go-to-the-shrine, you-know-everything-tell-me-how-to-live-my-life kind of thing. What I'm talking about here is what is commonly called "information interviewing." And you can do it with almost anyone.

The true efficacy of seeking advice and counsel can be clearly seen when you look at recent college graduates or people making career changes. There are literally thousands of occupational titles in the job market. Most of us know about seven of them. When new grads set out into the uncharted waters of the "real world," they always get there safer and quicker (and drier) when they seek help from knowledgeable friends and acquaintances.

Seek Opportunities to Demonstrate Your Capabilities

It's important to do good work, but you gotta blow your own horn once in a while. You have to look for opportunities to be noticed by those people with whom you can and should maintain strategic relationships.

I once consulted with a shopping mall that precipitously lost its leasing agent. Leases in the works and leads on businesses needing space were left dangling. The company's marketing secretary had close and frequent contact with the leasing agent, and though she didn't have his experience, she was familiar with the job. So, when she offered to take over the spot temporarily, upper management was delighted.

She was very good at sorting out the details and getting the lessors to agree to the standard lease wording. She had no problem getting help with things that needed to be negotiated. She insisted on sitting in on those negotiations, and at night she studied for her real estate license.

By the time the mall's managers got around to hiring the leasing agent's replacement, the marketing secretary had her license and had proven her abilities. It's little wonder they kept her right where she was and made the job permanent.

Here's another example: When a spice company I'd worked with called on its employees to help out with the company Christmas party, one of the administrative assistants stepped forward with the idea of putting together a special blend of peppercorns and having them custom wrapped for the employees as favors. The bosses loved the idea, and the administrative assistant managed to complete the project on time, within budget, using only in-house help.

He not only demonstrated his ability to get the job done; he also demonstrated his influence in the company by getting a number of different departments to help him with the project.

See, cultivating strategic relationships isn't as slimy as you thought it was. That's the good news. The not-so-good news is that it takes a lot of work. But as with anything worthwhile in this life, you have to put something in if you ever expect to get anything out.

Some people move through life as if they're running the gauntlet, pushing themselves for every last bit of performance. They get their satisfaction from knowing that they have lived through one ordeal and moved on to the next.

HAROLD BLOOMFIELD

Sustainable Motivation
How to Get Off the Emotional Roller Coaster

Y ou could say a lot of things about the sales profession, but none would be truer than this: It has its ups and downs. One month you're beating your quota like a rabid dog, the next you're wondering whether you'll have to sell your car to make your mortgage payment. Today your customers are naming their children after you; tomorrow it's "Brigid who?" This morning your product or service is hot as a headline; this afternoon it's yesterday's news.

Few professions are so inherently fraught with rejection, so laden with vicissitudes, so subject to extremes of fortune— except possibly acting and writing. And just as in those two endeavors, salespeople have to be "up" to do their jobs well. So what if your fourteen-year-old daughter came to the breakfast table sporting a tattoo, your spouse wants to take separate vacations this year, and the IRS called to remind you about next week's audit. Too bad. You've got sales calls to make. The show must go on or the commission checks won't go out.

And unlike most other professions, the road doesn't get any flatter when you *do* do your job well. Let's say you're a top performer, a real rainmaker. You're out there killing them every day. Quota? You don't need no stinking quota! You passed yours weeks ago. You're not just running with the big dogs, you're eating their spleens. Only now your peak numbers from last year have become your *baseline* numbers for this year. If you could move 10,000 units then, with a little extra effort you ought to be able to ratchet that up to 12,000. Never mind that you pulled out all the stops last year, ignored your health and your family, and did nothing but *work*. That sounds like a *personal* problem to me. Don't you have calls to make?

In other words, most salespeople I know are under relentless pressure. Let's set aside for the moment what this hamster wheel says about what passes for sales training and management in this country. (But only for the moment.) My point isn't to sing an ode to this country's beleaguered sales forces, though they have undoubtedly earned a song or two. What I'm pointing out here is that salespeople are used to motivating themselves and coping on an ongoing basis with powerful external and internal forces that can sabotage their performance. Most, it's sad to say, don't do this very well. They get hooked into the rah-rah sales guy stuff and the smile training only to find themselves on an emotional roller coaster, lurching up and down with the inevitable and even predictable cycles of the job.

But there are those sales pros who not only maintain a high level of performance but also continue to find a great deal of satisfaction and outright joy in their work. These are people who have managed to integrate into their work and personal lives a set of practices and behaviors that create *long-term sustainable motivation*. They have found a way to get off the carnival ride and to plant their feet on some terra that's a little more firma. And most of them are unstoppable.

That's what this chapter is about. You won't find any smile-training here, no rah-rah sales guy stuff, and no sales retreat rhetoric: nothing that would put you back on your particular hamster wheel. This chapter is not about how to *look* motivated. It's about going deeper and accessing your real power. It's about ferreting out the habits and behaviors that are sabotaging not just your work but all aspects of your life and replacing them with powerful tools that will help you level out that roller-coaster ride. It's not about numbing anxiety; it is about experiencing the joy of living.

This is the stuff neither Mom nor my sales manager ever told me, but that, through a combination of luck, great mentors, lots of reading, and years of banging my head against the wall, I finally figured out. I hope it spares you the bumpy head.

Sustainable Motivation

My dictionary defines motivation as "incentive, drive, stimulation of interest, inspiration." In another entry, it's called "the definite and positive desire to do things." I like both of these definitions, but I like the latter one better. Motivation is *definite*, it's *positive*, and it gets us to *do* things. In other words, motivation involves action. Just wanting to do something requires no motivation, nor does thinking we ought to. Motivation is the force that drives us to *act*, to *move*. "Movement" lives in the very root of the word.

To understand what I mean when I talk about *sustainable motivation*, you have to look at another word in that definition: *desire*. You cannot sustain motivation without it. And the funny thing about desire is that it can only come from within.

Sustainable motivation is the internal battery that keeps us moving toward our goals over time, despite the distractions and frustrations that life puts in our way. It cannot be diminished by circumstances outside ourselves, because it is internal. It doesn't depend on a sunny day; clouds cannot darken its luster.

Most of what we think of when we hear the word "motivation" is temporary, and it's usually used in a reactive context (more on that later). The sales manager looks at last month's numbers and decides he's going to have to "motivate" his crew. Typically, he'll turn to two "motivators": *fear* and *reward*. I mentioned the movie *Glengarry Glen Ross* earlier. There's a scene in that film that demonstrates how both of these "motivators" are typically used. The new sales manager comes in to kick butt and to take names, and he sets up a new sales contest: First prize is a Cadillac; second prize is a set of steak knives; third place is you're fired. Heartwarming and *soooo* effective.

Coaches do the same thing, though thankfully not all of them, as though motivation was something you could thump into somebody's head if you pound hard enough. Parents offer their children bicycles and CD players for good grades. Teachers promise field trips or threaten long detention. Family members and friends plead, cajole, and cry.

With all the best intentions in the world, we throw devices and systems at our unmotivated charges. Companies spend millions on feel-good seminars and "programs" to get their people in gear. I've seen any number of bizarre attempts to motivate employees. My favorite is the one in which the manager buses the team out to the woods, where they spend the weekend shooting paint pellets at each other. How on earth this will help Joe or Sally deal with a major client's decision to dump them for a competitor, I do not know.

But the biggest problem—the inherent problem—with all of these strategies is that they are *external*. Consequently, any resulting motivation is temporary at best. Once Johnny has that bike, he asks the inevitable question, "What will you give me next? A car?"

The truth is, no one can really motivate another person. Not for long, anyway. The drive to accomplish something has to come from inside if it is to be sustained. The above kinds of temporary strategies are literally repulsive. You know what I mean if you've ever been at the hands of a salesperson trying to win a trip to Hawaii on your nickel. Everything is amped up, artificial, and superficial. She's out to take what she can get from you, and you know it. And you can't get away from her soon enough.

But sustainable motivation is very attractive, even magnetic. There's *energy* there. People are drawn to internally motivated people. They are positive and productive as employees and generous and giving as friends and spouses. The drive behind their actions comes from a long-term commitment and realistic self-assessment, and it is generated by deep personal convictions. These are people who are never about making that particular sale; these are people who are living well.

And because their motivation comes from within them-selves, from inside, it is sustainable and will see them through the good times and the bad. That's one of the things that makes them so attractive: They don't get thrown when the deal goes south. Bumps in the road don't become barriers to their goals.

When you create sustainable motivation in your life, you don't crumble when you get laid off. You don't die when the interview goes badly. Your internal battery keeps you moving toward your goal. I mean, what good is a motivation strategy that only works when things are going your way? Think of sus-tainable motivation as your psychic Energizer bunny. It'll keep you going, and going, and going . . .

Responsive Versus Reactive

So the good news is the bad news: It's all up to you. There's some work to do here, but it is definitely *do*able and well worth the effort. But the way in which you approach the six basic components of sustainable motivation, which I've outlined on the next few pages, is almost as important as the components themselves. What I'm talking about here is the difference between being *responsive* and *reactive*.

No one's life is without ups and downs. To paraphrase the bumper sticker, stuff happens. You can't stop it, and you have to respond to it. What you *don't* have to do is *react*.

The difference between reacting and responding to events in your life is literally the difference between a reflexive act and thoughtful action. The reflex is the first impulse: "I'm going to punch that loudmouthed creep right in the nose!" The response is the considered action: "I'm going to find out what's going on with that guy." Maybe the creep deserves a broken nose; maybe he needs some constructive criticism. Either way, you don't deserve to be sued or to go to jail for battery.

A reactive mind puts you at the mercy of events and circumstances. But the responsive mind digs in and takes charge. It's the difference between *reacting* and *responding*. Reacting is about jumping off the career cliff by quitting your job to "show" your boss. It's about spouting off to your coworkers when you think you've been treated unfairly only to alienate them forever.

Components of Sustainable Motivation

Since sustainable motivation can come only from within, it can't be about other people's goals. Therefore, the following basic components of sustainable motivation aren't particularly useful for tricking yourself into doing something you really hate. This isn't a gimmick; it's a way of living. To make it work, you're going to have to start by telling the truth about where you are and what you really want.

For example: Ben was a client of mine who, because his parents had insisted, went to medical school and became a doctor. He was a good doctor, worked hard, and achieved a certain amount of success. Then, at the age of thirty-four, he finally woke up, went off autopilot, and asked himself what he really wanted to do. It took some sacrifice, a lot of work, and more guts than I'm used to seeing, but he left medicine and became a folksinger—a highly successful folksinger. He told me that he had decided his sentence was finally up.

Sustainable motivation is also about ungritting your teeth and knowing that your life could be a lot easier if you'd just

Attitude Monitoring

The minute I walked into the sales manager's office, I knew he was stressed out. He was sweating, fidgety, gulping coffee and aspirin like they were champagne and caviar. He said he just wanted me to go over the basics with some of his salespeople. Every other sentence out of his mouth was, "We're not stressed here; everything's fine."

Later, during the breaks in my presentation, each of his salespeople managed to corner me. "So," they'd ask, "how bad is it? Are we going out of business?"

make some healthy choices. The energy that powers your actions is a precious thing. To nurture and maintain it, you must pay close attention to each of the following basic components of sustainable motivation.

Attitude Monitoring

People who possess the power of sustainable motivation pay attention to what they say to themselves. It's always amazing to me how easily our self-talk can get out of control and how very, very powerful it is. I'm ten minutes late for an appointment, and my mind is telling me I'm dog meat. I'm standing before a particularly unresponsive audience, and my mind is telling me I shouldn't be here.

Our minds are liars, and we can't trust them. It's not true that I was dog meat when I was late to that appointment, but

> The fact was that the company was doing fine. Yet through his unconscious communication, the sales manager was delivering a message of doom to his sales staff. The operation wasn't exactly employee friendly, and the newly promoted sales manager found himself having to lie to his people and jerk them around, and it was killing him. But rather than deal with his feelings, he just kept cranking, stayed aloof from the staff, and developed an ulcer.
>
> He was so out of touch with the way he was coming across that he was making things miserable for everyone else. No one would—make that *could*—believe him.

my body reacted as though I was. The adrenaline was pumping, my driving was less than safe, and when I got there, I was tired and stressed out. Yet after a few words of explanation all was well.

Salespeople do this kind of thing all the time. It's called *catastrophizing*. But it can be subtle, too, and it happens to everyone. There's that little voice in the back of your head, wondering whether you really deserve this job, even though the interview is going very well. Here comes that voice again, telling you that you look fat in that dress, all these people are smarter, you don't belong, you're going to fail.

It is, all of it, a lot of nonsense. You have to know in your heart that you deserve to succeed and to be happy, or you will be drawn inevitably to failure and unhappiness. Isn't that why they tell you never to look at the headlights of oncoming vehicles when you're driving on a two-lane highway at night? The crash may be louder, but the effects aren't all that different.

Most of the stress in our lives comes from our own thoughts. When we fail to check in on our own thoughts, it's like having a low-grade fever. It doesn't really knock us out, but we're just not at our best.

Take the time every day to notice the things you are telling yourself. Keep a journal of your self-talk. Write down the thoughts and the circumstances under which they came up. You'll probably find the same thing coming up over and over again. Once you begin to see your pattern, you can confront it with a more reasonable counterargument.

Remember: This isn't about covering up with smiley talk. Tell the truth about yourself. But don't turn into your worst enemy. If your self-talk is negative, try changing your circumstances. Take a break, go for a walk, laugh. It's your mind that's doing the talking, but you don't have to listen.

When your attitude needs adjusting, try one of the following suggestions.

Cultivate a One-Day-at-a-Time Philosophy

This is about being in the moment and not filling your head with future thinking. It's about being present and sloughing off distracting, often debilitating, worries about what might happen next. It's about not being attached to outcomes. If you work on this one, you will develop the ability to focus completely on each individual sales contact or interview.

Taking it one day at a time says, "I'm going to give this my best shot, but this is not me. This is only what I'm doing right now, not who I am. I'm more than this, and I'll go on from here."

Play Your Winners

This involves taking a little inventory of things you've got going for you; counting your blessings, so to speak. Unfortunately, most of us focus on the things in our lives that don't seem to be working. I suppose it's a survival reflex. I mean, if it ain't broke, you don't have to fix it.

The problem is, paying too much attention to the problems in our lives creates a distorted view of things. So, you didn't get the job/promotion/sale. Does that really mean your life is terrible? What about your loving family, your good health, your full head of hair?

When I'm talking about this idea in a seminar, I usually ask people to write down five things in their lives that are working. I do this one myself. In fact, I jot these things on a three-by-five card that I keep with me and constantly update. When things start going south, I pull out the card, and it helps me get through the crisis of the moment.

Exercise

It's a classic stress reliever, and it works for bad attitudes, too. People who are exhausted, tired, or endocrinologically out of balance display their problems with their attitude. The connection between mind and body is widely accepted these days, even by the most conservative clinician. We've all had the experience of working things out in the gym. (If you haven't, I highly recommend it.)

Humor

Second only to exercise as a stress reliever, humor is a highly underrated tool for keeping things in perspective. You don't really have to take yourself so seriously. Frankly, and I say this

with all due respect, you're just not that important. Whatever you do (or don't do) today, the world will get along just fine. So lighten up.

Also, when you lose your sense of humor, you become very hard to be around. You don't have to be a joke meister—in fact, that's an extreme to which you don't want to go—but you add a lot to people's lives when you learn to appreciate the humor in things.

Overcoming the Fear of Pleasure

This is something that Americans have probably been dealing with since the Puritans landed. As you begin to listen more closely to your self-talk, you begin to hear very definite admonitions against . . . well, pleasure.

In his book *Inner Joy*, Harold Bloomfield, whom I quote at the beginning of this chapter, talks about this phenomenon. He asks the question, "Why must so much of life be a chore and so little of it be pleasurable?" The place to look for the answer, he says, "is not in what you do, nor in dogma about living, but in your basic attitude about pleasure and your own potential for abundant enjoyment of living."

I believe that the more easily we can experience pleasure, the better we feel about ourselves and the easier it is to stay motivated. I'm not talking about abandoning discipline for a profligate life of hedonism. I'm talking about lightening up!

About the effects of pleasure and the ability to experience it, Bloomfield goes on to say:

> Physically, pleasure improves circulation and increases energy. The emotional effects include greater self-esteem, increased self-confidence, and a generally sharper mind. Spiritually, enjoyment enhances your appreciation of your

blessings and contributes to a brighter outlook. Experiencing pleasure also allows you to have compassion for others when they are suffering. Pleasure is a source of strength to help others and contribute to the world.

What is our problem in this country? We all say we want to feel good, to enjoy our lives, to be fulfilled, yet very few of us will ever admit to liking our lives. It's as though we'll be punished for having too much fun.

But I believe, to paraphrase Mr. Bloomfield, that pleasure is not harmful, that it's nature's way of saying, Way to go! Sure, there are excesses in pursuit of pleasure, and I'm not advocating that approach to life. But if you can't enjoy the ride, there's really little point in getting on this train. The last stop is the same for everybody.

Selective and Screened Input

You can and must decide what kinds of media messages you let into your life. I don't mean that you should cancel your newspaper and put your head in the sand. This is not a don't-worry-be-happy strategy. But you cannot ignore the effects of the intensity of today's information onslaught on your ability to cope with life.

If you expose your weary mind every night to the horrors of the eleven o'clock news, you shouldn't be surprised to wake up feeling exhausted and fearful. You have to ask yourself, "Is this making me better informed, or is it just making me crazy?"

The Rodney King beating is a case in point. The tape of the event was broadcast on the nightly news, TV news-magazines, and talk shows over and over again until most of America could see the batons coming down on that man's head in their sleep. The sheer repetition of the clip amplified the event for millions. Were they better informed by allowing the

If It Feels Good, Let It

He'd been a coach for thirty-five years, and he loved it. He got to school by 6:00 every morning. He watched the boys he'd coached grow up to be responsible fathers, community leaders, and good, honest men. He never hesitated to tell you about his work. If you'd let him, he'd talk about it for hours. "It makes my life worthwhile," he'd say.

The coach was never swayed by the naysayers who told him his job was a dead end or the cynics who accused him of reaching the limits of his abilities. The business of

brutality of that event into their homes night after night? I say they were not. Were they made more fearful and anxious? Oh, you betcha.

Some news stories resonate more with us than others. When Polly Klaas was kidnapped from her home, I'm sure every parent of a twelve-year-old girl felt the impact of that event. If you're an assembly-line worker, news of blue-collar layoffs will affect you more than news of white-collar layoffs.

How are you going to function effectively in a sales role when your head is full of fear and worry generated by overexposure to events that will have little or no actual impact on your life? You're trying to convince a coworker to join your food drive while you're worrying about layoffs. You're trying to put your best foot forward at a job interview while images of street brutality dance in your head.

his life was coaching boys, and he allowed himself to enjoy it.

There's nothing quite so compelling as someone who genuinely enjoys their work. The coach was the best salesman the school could have, and he did it effortlessly. Being around him even made *me* like teenagers.

The message here is this: It's not just about finding work you love; it's also about giving yourself permission to enjoy it once you find it. Always allow yourself to acknowledge the pleasure a job gives you. It'll enhance your job performance and your life.

We need to think about what programs we watch on television, what books and magazines we read, what images we fill our lives with. We need to think through what time of day we expose ourselves to potentially disturbing events. And we need to notice when all this stuff is getting to us!

It is your responsibility to balance the types of messages you allow into your head. Sometimes, it's just better for you to shut off the noise for a while, get some alone time, put on some classical music, and give yourself a chance to regenerate.

Nutritious Friends

By "nutritious" friends, I mean people who are supportive, nurturing, and *effectively* judgmental—free enough of the constraints of misplaced emotion that they can recognize your potential and see where you as an individual can go. I'm not talking about adoring fans, hangers on, or cult members. Simply put, surround yourself with people who will feed your dreams, not starve your spirit (more on this in Chapter 7).

Organized, Supportive Physical Environment

In the *Power of Purpose*, Richard Leider points out the benefits of an "organized physical environment that is as simplified as it can possibly be."

Clutter and a hectic life are bound to wear you down. Life is crazy enough. You don't need the details to make you crazier. In fact, I don't know anyone who's saying, "Gee, I just don't have enough energy-sapping details to deal with." Yet very few of us do anything to cut down on those details and to simplify our lives.

I'm not talking Thoreau simple. You don't have to bag the rat race and set a lean-to by a pond in the woods to get the benefits of streamlining your situation.

If the house is driving you crazy, get a housekeeper. If your self-talk starts screaming, "I can't afford it!" that's when you should ask yourself, "What is your sanity worth?" If you don't have time to iron your shirts, take them to the cleaners. You might be able to change your own oil, but isn't it worth a few bucks to let someone else deal with it? My husband has a neat trick that simplifies his life: He has a standing haircut appointment. It's in his calendar, and he never has to think about it. Every five weeks he shows up, and he always looks good.

Then there are the folks who decide, "Okay, this week I'm going to lose ten pounds, switch jobs, get a divorce, and move to a better neighborhood." (I'm serious; that's a real example.) These folks are just sabotaging themselves and their motivation. There are only so many hours in the day. The idea is to use them well, not cram them full of activity.

Life Choices

Creating sustainable motivation is about making life choices. When you monitor your attitude, overcome your fear of pleasure, screen out toxic stimuli, surround yourself with nutritious friends, organize your environment, and fill your life with challenges, you are making a commitment to yourself and to your own personal development and effectiveness—a commitment that goes far beyond the smile training most salespeople are used to. How you treat yourself sets the standard for other people, because people learn twice as much from your example as your advice. These life choices aren't always easy, but they are worth the effort.

Life is either a daring adventure, or it's nothing.

HELEN KELLER

Coping with Change
It's a Cope-or-Crash Situation

B
ill is the president of his own company, a very smart man, and a friend of mine. He bought his company, which builds loading devices for barges, about twenty years ago. Bill recalls the man he bought the company from as "a totally burned out old guy with no more ideas and no energy who just wanted out of the business."

Recently, Bill and I were having lunch, and he told me about some changes he was making in the way he ran his company. They were fairly radical, and I was interested in learning why he had decided, after twenty years, to make those kinds of changes.

He told me about a meeting he'd had with one of his salesmen about a month earlier. The younger man was trying to tell him about some important changes in the market and some ideas he had about improving the business, but Bill just didn't want to hear about it. The young salesman became angry and told Bill that he and a number of the other salesmen were tired of not being listened to and were thinking of leaving the company.

"That was when it hit me," Bill said. "Twenty years ago, I was the one with all the energy and all the new ideas. But I had gotten stale. I had become the old guy I had bought the business from. I was about to drive away the best sales staff in the business. And for the first time in my life, I didn't know what to do."

Bill felt naked, standing there with the young salesman. He didn't have any quick answers for him. "But I took out my business card," he told me, "and I saw that I was still president of the company. I knew the salesman wasn't trying to put me down or to say I was in the way. He was just trying to tell me that I didn't know what was going on and that I should find out. I could see it was a cope-or-crash situation."

Bill decided not to crash. He didn't beat himself up over the situation or fire the insolent young man, either of which he could easily have done. And he didn't go on with business as usual. Instead, he listened.

Later, he hired professional consultants to talk with his employees, suppliers, and customers about what was really going on in his company and to help him come up with some new management strategies. The day after our lunch, he traveled to Manila with the young salesman to call on a customer himself—something he hadn't done in over ten years.

But the most important thing Bill did, for himself and for his company, was to accept *change*.

The Times They Are a . . . Well, You Know

Let's talk about change. I don't know about you, but I've heard that word so much lately—in the last presidential election, in the media, from high-tech pundits and prognosticating futurists—that I'm more than a little tired of it. In fact, if I were to be completely honest here, I'd have to say I'm sick to death of it.

"Change is everywhere."

"You can't stop change."

"Life is change."

Yuck!

What I want is something I can count on to be *un*changing. I want every American I talk with to speak at least one language in common with me. I want to know that the things my kids are studying in school today won't be obsolete by the time they hit the job market. I want to know for certain that nothing is going to replace CDs. I want to know, once and for all, what the heck I'm supposed to call Russia!

Unfortunately, that's just not the world I live in. The world I live in is a maelstrom of change unlike anything seen before in human history. Shifting, swirling, ebbing, flowing; new immigrant groups, different sexual orientations, unexpected family structures, mind-boggling technologies; I'm getting seasick just writing all this down!

No matter what I want, no matter how much I may long for simpler times, the world is complicated and getting more so almost daily. Fully half the things I learned in college are obsolete. Many of the skills with which I first entered the work world are no longer in demand. And who are these people with whom I'm working? Every day I'm confronted by a spectrum of colors and cultures with which I'm not always that comfortable.

So who said I'm supposed to be comfortable? As my friend from New York would answer, "Nobody, that's who."

The simple and utterly unavoidable fact of life in the world today is that things *are* changing. We are all hurtling at breakneck speed toward an uncertain future in which work and family structures may be unrecognizable, the American workforce will include people from very different backgrounds, and the things we will be called upon to do haven't even been imagined yet.

(As of this writing, the number-one employer in the United States is Manpower Temporary Services Agency; the job market has been changed forever.)

I know that if I want to survive and thrive in this storm of vicissitude, I've got to change with it. Not my morals or my fundamental beliefs, of course, but certainly my skills and my expectations.

It's a cope-or-crash situation.

My role models for coping effectively with change invariably come from the sales profession. You've probably seen that elaborate series of MCI television commercials in which a venerable old publishing house is installing a state-of-the-art telecommunications computer system. Some of the crustier editors are reluctant even to plug in their computers. But the sales guys are all for it. "It's about time!" they say.

It's fiction, I know, but there's a lot of truth in it, too. There's something about really good salespeople; they do better with change than almost any other group I can think of. The really effective ones are very adaptable types. They're never overwhelmed by change. They're used to dealing with new products and services, new customers and emerging markets. For them change is not something to be liked or disliked; it's just the way things are. Many have even made change into an ally.

I can't think of a more important sales skill to incorporate into our everyday lives.

I Don't Wanna and I Don't Hafta

Some people react to my admonitions about change with resentment and anger. That's okay. Change is hard. But if you let your resentments lead you to blindness, if they keep you from seeing the realities of the situation, you could find yourself obsolete and left behind, wondering what the heck happened. I mean, you wouldn't expect many people to find employment as blacksmiths nowadays. Yet I'm sure that 100 years ago the smithies would have resisted the notion that in a few years most people would be giving up horse-drawn transport for automobiles, trains, and trolleys.

The idea here is to *understand* how much the world is changing and how unlikely it is that things will ever go back to the way they were in some mythical "good old days." Here are some statistics from the U.S. Census Bureau that should bring what I've been talking about into clearer focus:

Thirty Years Ago

- The average worker was white, male, and about twenty-nine years old.

- Women generally worked in the home.

- When women did work, they were usually teachers, nurses, or support staff.

- Disabled workers were not generally seen in the workplace.

- *Gay* meant happy and carefree.

- One advertising message generally fit all customers.

Maybe You Should Do Windows

Lana's company and her role in it were changing. Business had slackened, and the competition had stiffened, so instead of sitting at her desk all day long taking orders, her bosses needed her to make three sales calls a week. "The way the market is going," they told her, "we really need everyone to help bring in business." They sent her to sales seminars, they gave her in-house training, but she was intractable: "I don't do windows, and I don't do *sales*." Her employers wanted to keep her. She'd been with the company for many years.

By the Year 2000

- The average worker will be forty years old.
- Two-thirds of the new entrants into the workforce will be women.
- Minority shoppers will have an annual spending power of $650 billion, more than the current GNP of Canada.
- Over $900 million will be spent on advertising aimed at minority groups.

You may not wanna, but you absolutely hafta.

It's clear, then, that change is being thrust upon us, but sometimes we *want* to make changes. We make a conscious decision to lose weight, to learn a language, to become computer literate, to make new friends, or to practice public speaking. Sometimes, as managers, supervisors, parents, or community leaders, we find ourselves becoming change agents, facilitating changes in

But she wouldn't adapt with the operation, so they let her go.

Today Lana spends eight hours a day in front of a CRT. She says she's happy there, but she can't be happy about losing her seniority and all the benefits the other company offered.

The bad news is that there are an amazing number of Lanas out there. In fact, business managers tell me her attitude is epidemic. The good news is that the reluctance of these folks to adapt to changes in their work situations makes more room for the rest of us.

others. Are these changes any easier to cope with? I don't think so. To me, change is change, whether we choose it or it chooses us. The idea is to embrace the most effective coping strategies, the ones that make the most of each individual situation.

The Truth About Change

As I've said before, the most important truth about change is that it is inevitable and unavoidable. That said, here are five more "truths" about change:

1. *Change is part of a process of continual improvement.*

This isn't to say that all change results in or from improvement. The cumulative effect of all the change in our lives—one hopes—is that we become more savvy, less reactive, and better able to take what seem like unrelated changes and combine them into something valuable. All change may not be good, but all the squirming and wriggling we do as individuals and as a society—the inevitable *movement* that results in change—is about growth, which sooner or later leads to improvement.

Losing track of the practical desirability of change, or, as is more often the case, invalidating importance in the process of continual improvement, can have wide-spread deleterious effects on individuals and society. Nowhere is this danger more evident than in our schools. The new campus of the University of California at Monterey Bay will be built on a model of "community-based, collaborative" learning, which to us locals is education-speak for "real-world learning in a job setting." Contrast that with *Popular Science* magazine noting in a recent article on education that Benjamin Franklin could walk into most elementary classrooms today and feel perfectly at home. The adherence to traditional teaching methods and the material is identical, in too many instances, to what he studied!

2. Change is incremental and requires transition time.

We're talking here about recognizing that you can't lose ten pounds overnight. As the great motto of Alcoholics Anonymous reminds us, "One day at a time." Sustainable changes are accomplished through a series of baby steps toward the changes, with plenty of tumbles along the way. When you are trying out a new skill or behavior, *give yourself some time to get used to the change*. Making the break from TV hound to nightly jogger is done one evening and one run at a time.

3. Communication diffuses the fear of change and provides the process for successful change.

It is an unfortunate fact of human nature that many of us expect the worst. In some of the companies with which I have worked, all changes are met with a predictable chorus of moans and groans. So, whether you are informing your family of a new career opportunity that will require a move or just driving across town to try out a new video store, the time you take to let others in on your thought processes and rationale will help to win them over to your side. One of the laws of communication is "You can't not communicate." Sometimes the less said, the more resistance you create.

4. Reaction to change is highly personal.

It's effortless to some and traumatic to others. Although it isn't certifiably genetic, it is true that some people will always want to be the first ones to try the new ice cream flavor, apply for the new position, or line up for the latest fad haircut. Others will hang on to the tried-and-true fashion statements established in their high school years.

One size does not fit all when it comes to coping with change. Find out how resistant you personally are to change and give yourself the time and the permission to choose the changes in your life, so you can have more success with them.

5. Coping with change is a crucial self-management skill.

The self-management skills that tend to get the most ink these days are *time* and *stress* management. However, managing the amount and intensity of the changes you are coping with is something only you can do for yourself. Even though our society is based on instant gratification in so many ways, your personal discipline in choosing and strategically "folding" changes into the dough of your life can make them a natural part of your maturing process. The keys here are self-knowledge and realizing that, whether you make the change now or later, making it consciously and purposefully will have a tremendous impact on the outcome.

Overcoming Change Anxiety

Wouldn't it be great if we could somehow delay the changes in our lives until we weren't so anxious about them? I think that's the unconscious strategy underlying much—but not all—of the resistance we experience when we are confronted with change. "I'll change when it doesn't scare me or make me uncomfortable." Unfortunately, that's like saying, "I'll have that appendectomy when my appendix heals up."

Only by confronting our anxiety can we ever hope to overcome it. Remember, change is, by its very nature, unsettling. When you make changes, you will be *uncomfortable*.

But you don't really have to be as uncomfortable as you might think. When you confront change directly, your worst fears almost never materialize. On those rare occasions when they do, you'll live through them. And remember, *not* changing can make us anxious, too, but in a far less productive way.

If you're feeling anxious about the changes in your life, try any of the following time-honored anxiety-reduction techniques:

- Call someone, as long as it's not someone who will give you permission to quit trying to change.

- Write about how awful it is in a letter to yourself or a journal.

- Exercise; it is the number-one weapon against anxiety.

- Go inside yourself with prayer or meditation.

- Read books on the subject of relaxation.

- Try dealing with just a piece of the change rather than trying to embrace the entire scope of it. (For instance, listen to a Spanish language radio station or check out the Spanish language soaps on TV before signing up for a semester-long Spanish course.)

Another way of dealing with change anxiety is with a pre-emptive strike. In other words, since your life is bound to be full of discomfiting changes, why not keep yourself flexible enough to cope with them on an ongoing basis?

I recommend a number of Jane Mitzer's "flexercises" for this purpose:

- Recall and examine past changes with which you have coped successfully.

- Make a deliberate change (practice makes perfect).

- Connect with different people.

- Give up trying to control the uncontrollable (practice going with the flow).

- Try something you'd "never do" (hire someone without a college degree; buy an American car).

- Take a physical risk (rock climbing, water skiing, bungee jumping).

- Literally *flex* your body (again, exercise is the greatest anxiety reliever).

A Better Baggage Handler

Change is difficult enough all by itself, but we tend to make it worse with additional fears, expectations, and resistance of our own. Some people call them filters or blind spots, but I prefer Dr. Judith Sills's *baggage* metaphor. She talks about three different kinds of baggage we carry with us into every new situation.

Behavioral Baggage

This includes our bad habits—all those guilty pleasures, devastating attachments, and knee-jerk responses that endanger our health, interfere with our productivity, and sometimes offend the people we would most like to impress. These are often centered around drugs, alcohol, cigarettes, food, television, or spending, among others.

Belief Baggage

This refers to any unexamined values, beliefs, or assumptions that make us sadder, more anxious, more frightened, or weaker. A few examples: "Nice girls don't talk about money"; "Men fix things"; "Women are nurses; men are doctors."

Emotional Baggage

This has to do with pieces of our past that interfere with our pleasure and productivity in the present. Our parents are the main focus of these types of feelings. But a former spouse or lover, a sibling, or another family member can also generate an impressive amount of intrusive emotional baggage.

The biggest source of emotional baggage, Sills says, is the secrets we keep. I couldn't agree more. A secret is not simply a truth withheld. It is a truth that requires energy to guard. It has very intense emotion attached to it, often feelings of guilt, shame, triumph, domination, or despair. Sills writes, "There is an old rule in family therapy: A family is only as sick as its secrets. In the same way, an individual's secrets are an excellent measure of his or her emotional baggage."

No wonder change is so tough!

We can lighten our loads of excess baggage little by little by learning to recognize and resist what Sills calls our "ruling passions." She defines *ruling passion* as the central need of the core drives and instincts around which we have built our personalities. Satisfying that need, she says, is an ongoing, and not always conscious, activity.

It's not always easy to recognize our ruling passions, let alone overcome them. Old habits, as they say, die hard. In my own case, it was developing the adult capacity for *saving money*. Argh! I didn't have an ant example when I was growing up; my parents were the quintessential grasshoppers, living from paycheck to paycheck, so saving was a skill I had to *learn*.

The good news is that you don't have to dump all your baggage to see big changes in your life. Drop a few carry-ons, and coping with change gets a lot easier. You're more open and less inclined to add anxiety-producing meanings to otherwise neutral events. Lose the garment bag, and you have that much more energy to deal with change head on; dump the steamer trunk, and you can really *tango*.

Taking the Initiative

One of the biggest mistakes I see people make when they set out to make conscious changes in their lives is taking on too many changes at once. In a way, it's not their fault. We're constantly bombarded with messages that tell us we *can* do it all. It's what Shad Helmsteddar calls "the myth of everybody else is happier than I am." If everybody else is doing it, there's something wrong with me. But nothing could be further from the truth.

There's also a notion out there that we have some specific changes we have to make, and once we've made them, we'll be fine and won't need to make any more.

Neither notion is true, and what's more, both make change that much harder. Remember, change takes time, it causes discomfort, and it's part of an ongoing process that never ends.

Therefore, the first and most important step in any coping strategy is *prioritization*. It may be true that you need to become computer literate, quit smoking, learn a language, make new friends, lose weight, and get a new job, but you simply can't do all of these things at once. If you shove too many things into the pipe, it's going to get clogged. To keep things flowing, you have to break things down into bite-sized pieces.

The key here is to identify those changes that directly affect you—your financial, social, emotional, and spiritual success—and then face them squarely. In the end, you will not merely cope with them but capitalize on them as well.

So be strategic. You can't change everything at once. Ask yourself, "What would give me the most for my efforts? What would solve my biggest problems or make my life better?"

Facilitating Change

After years of struggling with an old-fashioned, multiline telephone system, a credit union I work with installed a new voice-mail system to better accommodate the needs of its customers. The new system enabled them to take messages from members without having to put them on hold, and for the first time in years phones weren't constantly ringing in the offices. The system was added to improve member service, and the plan seemed like a good one.

But there was a problem: Many longtime employees hated the new system, and some of the customers were highly resistant to it, too. During the first few weeks after the system had been installed, absenteeism went way up, and there were instances of sabotage.

It's a given that people will resist change. But this fact is often forgotten in the rush to establish that new procedure, hustle the equipment to the new location, or get that new system on-line. When you find yourself in the position of imposing a change on others, keep the following in mind:

1. *Clear up any misconceptions.*

Vacuums create rumors; rumors are created to fill vacuums. And it's all about fear. If you're the receptionist and your job is to answer phones, and suddenly the boss installs a new voice-mail system, what question do you suppose would be uppermost in your mind? How about, "Do I still have a job?" Take the time early on to let people know what's coming, to answer their questions, and to give them a chance to ventilate. There is going to be a certain amount of complaining about even a change as seemingly harmless as painting the office. It's normal. But it's better to get it all out up front and to clear up any misconceptions that might sabotage your plans.

2. *Develop opportunities for participation.*

The credit union could have introduced the new system on one or two lines, giving people a chance to experiment with it, use it for a while, and then go back to their old system when things got confusing. Don't expect a zero-to-sixty response. People just can't deal with it.

3. *Provide adequate support.*

Whatever you think is adequate support, double or even triple it. Overdo it. "What questions do you have?" "Here, let me show you again." "Hey, Bob, how did it go this afternoon?"

Really stay on top of how everybody's doing with the change. It always takes more support than you think it will.

And lose the we've-had-it-for-a-week-haven't-you-figured-it-out-yet attitude. They haven't. If they had, they'd be Stepford wives.

4. *Recognize that the change is in the people and not in the things.*

Okay, we've got this new phone system, but what we really have here is a new way for the staff to respond to the customers. That is an absolutely make-it-or-break-it concept. The real change is always in the people. Unless yours is a one-man show, you need them to implement your changes.

5. *Allow enough time for transition.*

Again, it's not how long you think it ought to take; it's how long it takes. Your people are probably coming from, "We have a phone system. It works. Why fix it if it isn't broken?" People need transition time.

6. *Foster a sense of organizational identity.*

Everybody in your group should be made to feel as though they're all in it together. You can't say, "Well, hey, Accounting has picked up this new system just fine. It's Marketing that's screwing up." Even if that's true, if you want your changes to go forward smoothly, you have to get everyone on the same team. It's about giving them the big picture.

7. *Recognize and discourage magical thinking.*

"Of course! If I weren't going through a divorce and all these problems at home, then they wouldn't be making all these changes at work." People really see themselves as the center of the universe and take things personally. Interest rates are going up because I just got this damned loan. It's raining because I just washed my car.

This "magical thinking" must be discouraged. You must communicate the reasons for the changes and make it clear wherever necessary that you're not out to get anybody.

When I talk about change with my mother-in-law, she uses an expression I like very much: "early days." She uses it when she's talking about marriage, parenthood, almost anything. As I understand it, she means that you're always in a new phase of whatever you're doing. Being married seven years is different from being married twenty years. Having toddlers is different from having teenagers.

We're always in those "early days." The trick is to make the most of them.

10

Maybe I'm just like my mother, she's never satisfied.

THE ARTIST FORMERLY KNOWN AS PRINCE

Good, Better, Best
Excellence Versus Perfection

I love T-shirts. I don't mean the plain white ones my husband buys in three-packs at Target, but the ones with logos and slogans on them. Maybe it's because I was raised in a military family and didn't get to wear them as a child, but I think they're fun, like temporary tattoos or a kind of legalized graffiti. But I also think they're important reflections of what's going on in the collective mind of our society. A thousand years from now, historians and archeologists digging back into the whys and wherefores of the twentieth century could learn a lot from a treasured T-shirt collection. (There's an argument to be made here for bumper stickers, too, but I'll save that for the next book.)

On Doing It "Right"

Caroline was trying to make a career change, but she was struggling. She was working as a Mary Kay rep with little success. The Mary Kay sales training is generally excellent, but it didn't seem to be helping Caroline. When she tried out her presentation on me, I began to see the problem. She'd start talking and then suddenly stop in the middle of a phrase. "Oh, wait, I didn't get that right." And then: "Oh, gosh, I'm not supposed to tell you that." And again: "Gee, at home in the mirror I had this down perfectly, just like they told me to." Her frustration was palpable.

The most common sartorial slogans I remember from my youth were about music, politics, or sex—or all three: "make love not war," "rock 'n' roll will never die," and "Never trust anyone over thirty." (That sounds like the sixties!) The fashionable catch-phrases that stand out in my mind today, however, reflect a very different preoccupation: "second place is the first loser," "he who dies with the most toys wins," and the ever popular "no fear." What these say to me about the dominant thinking in our society is worrisome. They seem to be espousing an all-or-nothing point of view. Either you're number one, or you're a zero. Striving is for losers. If you don't win, it wasn't worth the effort.

I'm all for cultivating a competitive spirit, and I'm very much in agreement with the idea that we should all work to

I talked with her and discovered that she was aware of her trouble with perfectionism. "Not only do I believe in perfection," she said, "but I've managed to drive my two sons out of my life by trying to make them perfect, too."

It all finally hit her when her youngest son was in his third year of college. She found herself on the phone, telling him exactly how much Tide to put into a load of laundry. "He told me to butt out of his life and hung up," she said tearfully. "I just wanted to make sure he was doing it right."

What a burden for both of them! How much better to give up the perfectionism and accept excellence.

improve ourselves and strive for excellence. Contentment for its own sake is not one of my goals. But I believe the kind of black-and-white value system I see emerging today is causing many of us to put pressure on ourselves that's not useful and in many cases is destructive. I believe it's causing many of us who strive for and achieve *excellence* to discount our achievements in a relentless and unfulfilling pursuit of *perfection*.

This chapter is about learning to tell the difference between excellence and perfection. It's about learning to recognize the damage black-and-white thinking can do and rising above it. I'm not promoting mediocrity here or trying to get anyone to accept less. What I'm trying for is something of a wake-up call that will alert the perfectionist in all of us to the true worth of our accomplishments.

You Don't Control the World

Salespeople are good examples of folks who face the excellence-versus-perfection trap on an almost daily basis. I've known effective salespeople with very high standards of performance but never a true perfectionist. Maybe it's the nature of the profession, the constant rejection, the inevitable changes. The ones who stay in the profession and really thrive get used to looking at a bigger picture than this or that particular sales call or specific nonsuccesses. Instead of spending their time analyzing every bump in the road, they just keep on driving until they reach their destinations. I think of them as the all-terrain vehicles of the business world.

It can be tough to maintain your perspective in the sales game. As I said in Chapter 8, the pressure is always on. For many salespeople, their top numbers this year become their baseline numbers for next year. "Yeah, yeah, that was good *yesterday*," their sales managers always seem to be saying, "but what have you done for me *today*?" Good never seems to be good enough.

Yet effective salespeople in particular, but also effective people in general, realize they don't control their managers, the marketplace, their customers, their spouses, their kids, potential employers, or the weather. They know that success is not about control. It's about stepping up to the plate, taking your best swing, and then going on to the next inning. To them it's a game of averages. They know that even when they're batting 500, they're missing half the balls thrown at them.

Our everyday selling skills kit wouldn't be complete without examining the difference between excellence and perfection.

The Power of Perfection

One of the things that makes it so hard for us to see the destructive power of perfectionism is that we value it so highly in this society. Remember the last time you heard someone described as a perfectionist? Was it used derogatorily? My guess is that it was said with admiration. The Hollywood director is called a perfectionist, and everybody nods, silently agreeing that he's hard to work with but secure in the knowledge that he produces wonderful films. The cabinetmaker is known for his perfectionism, and so his cabinets are highly valued. The manager is called a perfectionist, and everyone relaxes, understanding that she is someone who can be counted on. Perfectionists are neat, clean, punctual. They're dedicated to mastering their craft, doing very good work, never missing a beat.

What's wrong with all that? Nothing. But I don't think *perfectionist* is a word that really applies in the above cases. The director is an artist unwilling to compromise his vision. The cabinetmaker is a master craftsman with high standards. The manager may well be the most flexible member of the team. These are people who are striving for excellence, but are they striving for perfection? Are they slaves to unrealistic standards? I doubt it.

What exactly is the difference between excellence and perfection? Here's a comparative list that should answer that question. I compiled it over the years from a number of sources, including the many twelve-step programs out there and the contributions of savvy salespeople I interviewed for this chapter.

1. Excellence *is being willing to be wrong;* perfection *is needing to be right.*

When we have to be right, there's a tendency to cling to ideas and procedures. They may be outdated or just plain wrong (which kind of defeats the compulsion in the first place). But they're known and established and so possess a kind of legitimacy. Out of the need to be right, we find ourselves defending our positions instead of examining and reexamining them. Our thinking becomes calcified. You can very quickly make yourself obsolete with that kind of thinking.

When we give ourselves permission to be wrong, we also give ourselves room to grow. We free ourselves from calcified thinking and defensiveness, and we move readily with the changes that are so inevitable.

2. Excellence *is about taking risks;* perfection *is about fear of failure.*

Our need to be perfect can create all kinds of fear. The kind I see most often is fear of failure, which can leave us paralyzed and utterly unable to act.

To succeed we must act. By embracing risk—calculated, sensible, strategic risk—we free ourselves to act. When we let go of the need to succeed every time we try, we increase our chances of success in the long run.

3. *Striving for* excellence *makes us powerful; pursuing* perfection *makes us angry and frustrated.*

When we're pursuing perfection, we grasp at everything and absorb nothing. We continue to impose our expectations of how things *ought* to be on the way things *are*. We pit our unrealistic standards against reality, and many times we end up clinging again to the old and established and end up angry and frustrated.

When we strive for excellence, we're positive and full of energy. We have a great deal of power, because we're not struggling to impose our expectations on a given situation. We know that we can handle whatever new things come along. It will get easier and better.

4. Excellence *is spontaneous;* perfection *is con-trolled.*

There's an old Hebrew proverb that I especially like: "Man plans; God laughs." We can never be fully prepared for every contingency; we can only be prepared to *accept* the un-expected. If we're tight and clinging to our illusions of control, when the unexpected happens—as it absolutely must—we find we can't cope. And we can miss opportunities that may not come along again.

5. Excellence *is open and accepting;* perfection *is closed and judgmental.*

Remember Chapter 9? Of course you do, excellent reader that you are. If you haven't read it, you might stop now and take a peek. With the pace of change in our society that I discuss in that chapter, how could anyone fail to see the importance of remaining open and accepting, especially in the workplace?

That's what all of this diversity training is all about. Things aren't the way they were. People are different: different races, different cultures, different costumes. We have a whole genera-tion that's pierced and tattooed something awful.

If we impose our rigid judgments on people we don't understand, once again we will miss opportunities and impose a struggle in our work and our lives that is probably unnecessary.

6. Excellence *is about giving;* perfection *is about taking.*

One of the things I hope to change with this book is the common stereotype of the slimy sales guy. The guiding princi-ple of this approach is that sales is about making the other person's needs as important as your own. When we strive for excellence, that's exactly what we do. We create win/win situations wherever we can.

When we saddle ourselves with perfectionistic thinking, we often find ourselves in win/lose situations. We've got to make the sale, so everything else goes out the window.

7. Excellence *gives us confidence;* perfection *leaves us full of doubt.*

Perfectionism, at its essence, is a strategy of looking to an external "higher" standard. It's about comparisons, usually to an unachievable ideal. When we employ a perfectionistic strategy, we're always full of doubt. We know in our hearts that no one is perfect. Consequently, it's just a matter of time until we fail.

Striving for excellence is about doing a job well. That's something we can judge for ourselves. We don't need an outside standard. We know in our hearts what we can do, beyond invidious comparisons. Therefore, we tend to look to ourselves for confirmation. Since we're in charge, we're setting the standards; we're in control.

8. Excellence *is free flowing;* perfection *exists only under pressure.*

Striving for excellence is like dancing. We don't know exactly where we're going to move next, but we know the steps, and if we stay loose and respond to our partners, we know we'll get there. We don't have a diagram on the floor, but we can still manage to bring it all together without stepping on anyone's toes. And it's fun!

Perfection creates intense pressure to do things *right* and to make no mistakes. We find ourselves on the dance floor, but we're obsessed with putting our feet in exactly the right spots.

When our partners do something unexpected, something out of our control, we struggle. We fail to feel the music. We fail to respond to what's going on, in service of what *should* be going on.

9. Excellence *is about the journey;* perfection *is about the destination.*

If there is one point to make in this chapter, it is this one. The people who read my books aren't usually having trouble with motivation or hard work. Quite the contrary. Most of them are borderline workaholics—and a whole lot have crossed that border. But many fail to recognize the worth of their own accomplishments. They often shuttle from one destination (accomplishment) to another without ever noticing that the journey is what counts. That's where you live, between successes.

If you come away from this book with only one thing, it is my sincerest hope that it is this: Enjoy every step of the journey!

You're the One Keeping Score

I see excellence losing the battle with perfection most clearly in my consulting practice. Many of the people I talk to these days have gotten into the very dangerous habit of never being satisfied even when they *do* have the most toys. For them success is never enough, never like they thought it would be, never like it was *supposed* to be. Never right. Never *perfect*. For them the good has become the *enemy* of the perfect, an unsatisfying second place. And their lives have become infected with a poisonous discontentment with which they contaminate everything they touch.

Maybe worse, I've seen people using this black-and-white thinking as an excuse to sit on the couch in front of their television sets and channel surf their lives away. Or they use the inevitable setbacks we all experience to support their decisions to quit trying. "I didn't get that job, so I'm totally unemployable"; "I didn't marry *him*, so I'm totally unlovable"; "I don't look like Cindy Crawford/Marky Mark/Demi Moore/Mel Gibson, so I'm a total beast, and there's no point in taking care of myself." It's as though they're looking for ways to turn their lives into dog meat.

The question then becomes, Who's keeping score? Who determines how things are supposed to be? Who says what's good enough? Who decides what's perfect?

The answer, of course, is *you*.

"Are we the happiest family?" "Am I making as much money as I can?" "Am I the most highly thought-of member?" "Is mine the best car?" You are the one who decides the answers to these questions. You're the one who decides when good is good enough. And if you never put on the brakes, you're the one who creates your own little squirrel cage.

In her book *Real Moments*, Barbara DeAngelis talks about what an excellent striver she used to be. She would work ten-hour days and think, "Hey, I can do twelve." And then she would find herself putting in fourteen hours, and then sixteen. Besides the sheer exhaustion of it, what she finally found was that it didn't really matter how many hours she put in, or how well she did her work, or how much applause she received; it all meant nothing—because she wasn't doing any of the clapping.

Once you understand that you're the one keeping score, then you can back up, go for that bigger picture I was talking about before. You can notice, say, that you're not really enjoying your work. You can take a look at what's broken or out of balance in your life. And you can take steps to fix it.

Never a Beginner

One of the great dangers of pursuing perfection over excellence is that it can keep us from trying new things. The perfectionists I've known were particularly uncomfortable with the process of learning a new skill. Perfectionists want to do it right, which we all do in the end, I suppose, but they have a hard time with what venture capitalists call the startup phase. In other words, they lack the ability to be a *beginner*.

Whether it's skiing, developing computer skills, learning a language, or getting an advanced degree, black-and-white thinkers are impatient with themselves in the early stages of the process. This impatience can make the experience so awful that anyone would quit. Or, seen another way, their determination to get it right—their need to avoid making mistakes—keeps their noses buried in the manual long after they should have rolled up their sleeves and just dug in.

To get good at something, you have to be bad at it first. Trust me, you perfectionists out there; it's a rule. How good you eventually become at a given skill depends on factors such as the time available to you for practice, the quality of your training, your interest, and your natural talents. But there is no escaping the part where you're lousy. *You gotta be bad before you can be good.*

To a certain extent, we're all uncomfortable with the process of learning a new skill, whether or not we think of ourselves as perfectionists. I've found that understanding the different stages of the process has helped me to accept my early failures.

The Phony Feeling Phase

When you first begin practicing and using a new skill, it feels all wrong. It feels more like you're playing at it than actually doing it. It doesn't feel the way you thought it would, doesn't look the way it did when the pro demonstrated it, and the whole thing takes a heck of a lot of concentration and energy. It can even be embarrassing.

This is the toughest phase to overcome and where most perfectionists bail out. Heck, it's where most of us bail. But when we hang in there, we soon get to phase two.

The Uncomfortable Phase

At this phase, you're still lousy at your new skill, but you have the "rules" in place in your head. This is when you find yourself muttering, "Eye on the ball, eye on the ball" or "Listen more, talk less; listen more, talk less." Things feel more familiar, though you still can't seem to do anything right.

This is where perfectionists who hung in there through the phony feeling phase can be particularly impatient with themselves. After all, they hung in there through the beginning phases; why haven't they gotten this thing down yet? The temptation here, again, is to quit. But if they stick with it, they will eventually be rewarded with phase three.

The Skilled and Aware Phase

In this phase, you're finally getting it. You know what to do, and the motor responses are coming. You haven't exactly mastered the skill yet, but you're beginning to return your instructor's serves with some consistency, recognizing opportunities for active listening, actually understanding your teacher when she asks you something in French. You're beginning to experience the rewards of sticking with it.

Extreme perfectionists who manage to get to this phase may still have a tendency to give up. While they're beginning to get the hang of things, they still haven't gotten it *right*. Judgments about how quickly they should have learned the skill come into play. "Sure, I'm getting it, *finally*, but I've worked hard enough that I ought to be great at this by now. If it took me this long to get here, how long is it going to take to get really good?"

Though they've hung in there, they're progressing nicely, and have done a really excellent job, they're not satisfied. But they have to get past their dissatisfaction to make it to phase four.

The Integrated Phase

Eventually, every new skill becomes so much a part of us, it's hard to imagine ever not being able to do it well. It's as natural as reading or driving a car. This is the phase perfectionists want to get to right out of the chute. It's not so much that they don't understand the need to practice to excel at a skill; it's that they hate doing anything wrong.

We all have an intolerant little perfectionist inside us. If we don't put a leash on him or her, we'll never get through this natural process to the reward of true mastery.

In recent years researchers have mapped a pattern of progress through this skill-acquiring process that might surprise you. Most of us expect to get a little better at something each time we practice it, steadily improving in a straight, ascending line. Apparently, that's not quite how it works. Instead, as we practice a new skill, we remain at the same level for quite a while, then we briefly *get worse* just before we experience a noticeable improvement. We then stay at the new level, briefly get worse again, and then move up again. The pattern is plateau, worse, better, plateau, worse, better.

The bottom line for me in all this is, as I've said, to enjoy the journey. If we would all just see ourselves as works in progress—which, by any standard, we are—we could free ourselves of the limitations of perfectionism. And then nothing could keep us from the excellence we all deserve.

BIBLIOGRAPHY

Ash, Mary Kay. *Mary Kay—You Can Have It All.* Rocklin, CA: Prima Publishing, 1995.

Beck, Arthur C., and Ellis D. Hillmar. *Positive Management Practices.* San Francisco: Jossey-Bass, 1986.

Bernstein, Albert, and Sydney Craft Rozen. *Dealing with All Those Impossible People at Work: Dinosaur Brains.* New York: Ballantine Books, 1992.

Blanchard, Kenneth, and Norman Vincent Peale. *The Power of Ethical Management.* New York: Morrow, 1988.

Blanchard, Kenneth, and Don Shula. *Everyone's a Coach.* Grand Rapids, MI: Zondervan Publishing House and Harper Business, 1995.

Bloomfield, Harold H. *Inner Joy.* New York: Wyden Books, 1980.

Bolles, Richard N. *What Color Is Your Parachute?* (updated ed.) Berkeley, CA: Ten Speed Press, 1994.

Covey, Stephen R., A. Roger Merrill, and Rebecca R. Merrill. *First Things First.* New York: Simon & Schuster, 1994.

DeAngelis, Barbara. *Real Moments.* New York: Delacorte Press, 1994.

Doyle, M., and D. Straus. *How to Make Meetings Work.* New York: Playboy Paperbacks, 1976.

Drucker, Peter F. *Managing for Results.* New York: Harper & Row, 1964.

Frank, Milo O. *How to Get Your Point Across in Thirty Seconds or Less.* New York: Pocket Books, 1986.

Gandolfo, Joe, with Robert L. Shook. *How to Make Big Money Selling.* New York: Harper & Row, 1986.

Helmstetter, Shad. *What to Say When You Talk to Yourself.* New York: Pocket Books, 1982.

Johnson, Spencer. *One Minute for Myself.* New York: Avon Books, 1985.

Johnson, Spencer, and Larry Wilson. *The One Minute Salesperson.* New York: Avon Books, 1984.

Kearney, Elizabeth L., and Michael J. Bandley. *Everyone Is a Customer.* (2nd ed.) Provo, UT: Sterling Press, 1990.

Kieffer, George David. *The Strategy of Meetings.* New York: Warner Books, 1988.

Leider, Richard J. *The Power of Purpose.* New York: Ballantine Books, 1985.

Mackay, Harvey. *Swim with the Sharks Without Being Eaten Alive.* New York: Morrow, 1988.

McGrath Massie, Brigid, with John K. Waters. *What Do They Say When You Leave the Room?* Salinas, CA: Eudemonia Publications, 1991.

Naisbitt, John, and Patricia Aburdene. *Reinventing the Corporation: Transforming Your Job and Your Company for the New Information Society.* New York: Warner Books, 1985.

Peters, Thomas J., and Robert H. Waterman. *In Search of Excellence: Lessons from America's Best-Run Companies.* New York: Warner Books, 1982.

San Francisco Chapter of the National Association of Professional Organizers. *Organizing Options: Solutions from Professional Organizers.* San Francisco: NAPO, 1994.

Schneider, Benjamin, and David Bowen. *Winning the Service Game.* New York: Benjamin Schneider and David E. Bowen, 1995.

Sills, Judith. *Excess Baggage: Getting Out of Your Own Way.* New York: Penguin Books, 1993.

Slaby, Andrew. *Sixty Ways to Make Stress Work for You.* New York: Bantam Books, 1991.

Smith, Hyrum W. *The Ten Natural Laws of Successful Time and Life Management.* New York: Warner Books, 1994.

Stern, Frances Meritt, and Ron Zemke. *Stressless Selling.* Englewood Cliffs, NJ: Prentice-Hall, 1981.

Timm, Paul R. *Fifty Simple Things You Can Do to Save Your Customers, Your Business, and Your Job.* Salt Lake City, UT: Customer Satisfaction Strategies International, 1991.

Wujec, Tom. *Pumping Ions: Games and Exercises to Flex Your Mind.* New York: Doubleday, 1988.

Ziglar, Zig. *Top Performance: How to Develop Excellence in Yourself and Others.* New York: Berkeley, 1987.

INDEX

Small Business Today Guide to Beating the Odds

Hattie Bryant

Based on the popular public television series, *Small Business Today,* this timely book shows readers how to assess their strengths, decide on a business to start, find funding, and set up a business plan. This book provides the direction and advice needed by anyone presently self-employed or thinking about starting a small business. Hattie Bryant is the producer of the successful public television series *Small Business Today.*

Mary Kay—You Can Have It All

Mary Kay Ash

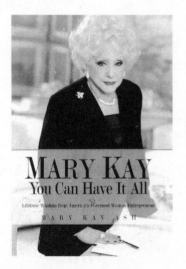

Mary Kay may be the most successful woman entrepreneur in the world today. Following her priorities—God first, family second, and career third—and some sound, savvy business strategies, she managed to create a multibillion-dollar international company as well as a fulfilling life that reflects her values. Mary Kay Ash is founder and chairman emeritus of Mary Kay Cosmetics Inc., listed among *Fortune's* Most Admired Corporations in America and boasting annual retail sales of more than $1.5 billion.

Success Secrets of the Motivational Superstars
Michael Jeffreys

This one-of-a-kind collection features interviews with sought-after leaders such as Anthony Robbins, Wayne Dyer, Les Brown, Tom Hopkins, Barbara DeAngelis, Art Linkletter, Brian Tracy—and many more. These are speakers who sell out 3000-seat auditoriums around the country—not because they can sing or act, but because they *communicate*. No book available today brings together the advice of so many top names in this field. Michael Jeffreys is a speaker, writer, and magician. He works with major corporations to inspire and teach their top managers.

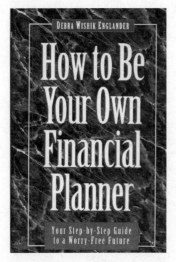

How to Be Your Own Financial Planner
Debra Wishik Englander

For those who already use a planner, broker, or other professional, this book will help ensure that they get their money's worth from the experts. For the novice, this book provides the basics of budgeting and how to make money earn more. Debra Wishik Englander is a highly recognized financial writer. She was head of the Book-of-the-Month Club's business book club and part of the editorial staff at *Money* magazine.

PRIMA PUBLISHING
P.O. Box 1260BK   Rocklin, CA 95677

USE YOUR VISA/MC AND ORDER BY PHONE
(916) 632-4400
Monday–Friday 9 A.M.–4 P.M. PST

I'd like to order copies of the following titles:

Quantity	Title	Amount
_____	_____	_____
_____	_____	_____
_____	_____	_____

Subtotal _____

Postage & Handling° _____
Sales Tax: 7.25% (CA); 5% (IN and MD); 8.25% (TN) _____
TOTAL (U.S. funds only) _____

Check enclosed for $ _____(payable to Prima Publishing)

HAWAII, ALASKA, CANADA, FOREIGN, AND PRIORITY REQUEST ORDERS,
PLEASE CALL ORDER ENTRY FOR PRICE QUOTE (916) 632-4400

Charge my ☐ MasterCard ☐ Visa
Account No. _____ Exp. Date_____
Print Your Name _____
Your Signature_____
Address _____
City/State/Zip _____
Daytime Telephone (___) _____

°Postage & Handling	
Purchase Amount:	Add:
$14.99 or less	$3.00
$15–$29.99	$4.00
$30–$49.99	$6.00
$50–$99.99	$10.00
$100 –$199.99	$13.50

Prices are subject to change.

Please allow three to four weeks for delivery.